THIRD EDITION

4A

Q

Skills for Success
LISTENING AND SPEAKING

Robert Freire | Tamara Jones

OXFORD
UNIVERSITY PRESS

UNIVERSITY PRESS

198 Madison Avenue
New York, NY 10016 USA

Great Clarendon Street, Oxford, OX2 6DP, United Kingdom

Oxford University Press is a department of the University of Oxford.
It furthers the University's objective of excellence in research, scholarship,
and education by publishing worldwide. Oxford is a registered trade
mark of Oxford University Press in the UK and in certain other countries

© Oxford University Press 2020

The moral rights of the author have been asserted

First published in 2020

2024 2023 2022
10 9 8 7 6 5 4

No unauthorized photocopying

All rights reserved. No part of this publication may be reproduced, stored
in a retrieval system, or transmitted, in any form or by any means, without
the prior permission in writing of Oxford University Press, or as expressly
permitted by law, by licence or under terms agreed with the appropriate
reprographics rights organization. Enquiries concerning reproduction
outside the scope of the above should be sent to the ELT Rights
Department, Oxford University Press, at the address above

You must not circulate this work in any other form and you must impose
this same condition on any acquirer

Links to third party websites are provided by Oxford in good faith and for
information only. Oxford disclaims any responsibility for the materials
contained in any third party website referenced in this work

ISBN: 978 0 19 490492 6   STUDENT BOOK 4A WITH IQ ONLINE PACK
ISBN: 978 0 19 490480 3   STUDENT BOOK 4A AS PACK COMPONENT
ISBN: 978 0 19 490540 4   IQ ONLINE STUDENT WEBSITE

Printed in China

This book is printed on paper from certified and well-managed sources

ACKNOWLEDGEMENTS

Back cover photograph: Oxford University Press building/David Fisher

The author and publisher are grateful to those who have given permission to reproduce the following extracts and adaptations of copyright material:
p. 5 from "Leadership isn't just for the boss" by CBC Radio-Canada, 31 July 2017. © CBC Radio-Canada. Reproduced by permission; p. 11 Hammett, Pete. "3 Ways to Break Out of Your Executive Bubble." Audio blog post. Leading Effectively. Center for Creative Leadership, 2007. www.ccl.org. Drawn from *Unbalanced Influence: Recognizing and Resolving the Impact of Myth and Paradox in Executive Performance*, Davies-Black Publishing, Copyright © 2007 Pete Hammett. Reproduced by permission; p. 35 from "Colour Schemes: How Colours Make You Buy" from Under the Influence with Terry O'Reilly, 10 May 2018, CBC Radio. © Terry O'Reilly. Reproduced by permission; p. 62 from "A lament for the sad state of financial literacy among young people" by CBC Radio-Canada, The Sunday Edition, 6 March 2016. © CBC Radio-Canada. Reproduced by permission; p. 154 adapted from "The Power of Serendipity" from CBS News Sunday Morning, 7 October 2007. © CBS News. Reproduced by permission of CBS News Archives; p. 180 from "Automation and Us" by CBC Radio-Canada, 5 October 2014, 6 March 2016. © CBC Radio-Canada. Reproduced by permission.

Illustrations by: pp. 81, 82, 96, 99 Mark Duffin; p. 73 Joe Taylor.

We would also like to thank the following for permission to reproduce the following photographs: **123rf:** pp. 5 (informal business meeting/Mark Bowden), 36 (BP logo/Alexandr Blinov), 57 (student/Antonio Diaz), 70 (parents holding infant/Mark Bowden), 83 (kerosene lamp/Oleksandr Kozak), 104 (Peking duck/Mikhail Valeev), 105 (drone/Goce Risteski), 119 (chocolate ice cream/Hans Geel), 155 (coffee beans/Ilja Generalov), 156 (GPS/Igor Stevanovic), 173 (popsicles/Jennifer Barrow); **Alamy:** pp. 2 (conductor and orchestra/imageBROKER), 11 (business meeting/MBI), 15 (colleagues working together/Albert Shakirov), 16 (John Donahoe/ZUMA Press, Inc.), 18 (student listening to podcast/Dan Grytsku), 22 (supervisor giving talk to employees/Hero Images Inc.), 30 (Agatha Christie/Everett Collection Historical), 32 (boy in messy room/Big Cheese Photo LLC), 38 (Owens Corning advertisement/Cal Sport Media), 49 (stressed woman/Andriy Popov), 52 (woman voting/Hero Images Inc.), 54 (Seijin no Hi celebration/dpa picture alliance), 62 (woman counting money/Hero Images Inc.), 78 (space rocket/Konstantin Shaklein), 104 (shark liver oil/BSIP SA), 108 (man assembling drone/Montgomery Martin), 109 (organic sign/David Angel), 113 (family walking/Carmen K. Sisson/Cloudybright), 135 (intern and supervisor/LightField Studios Inc.), 147 (women leaving college library/Adam Bronkhorst), 152 (abseiling in cave/Cavan), 154 (doctor examining x-ray/Blend Images), 156 (pacemaker/Phanie), (Velcro/Stocksnapper), 158 (magnetron/Aleksandr Volkov), 166 (brain injury/BSIP SA), (Phineas Gage/ART Collection), (skull graphic/BSIP SA), 168 (nomad with camel/Guillem Lopez), 170 (professor lecturing/Reeldeal Images), 172 (raised hands/Wavebreak Media ltd), 176 (man photographing nature/Cultura Creative RF), 177 (woman in deep sea submersible/SeaTops), 182 (doctor and patient/Hero Images Inc.), 190 (traffic/Don Bartell), 201 (man with personal assistant/Image navi - QxQ images), 203 (family on video call/Tetra Images, LLC); **Getty:** pp. cover (prismatic background of binary code/KTSDESIGN/SCIENCE PHOTO LIBRARY), 4 (woman with award/Hill Street Studios), 6 (restaurant manager and employee/andresr), 8 (boss and employee in shop/andresr), 13 (suggestion box/Randy Faris), 20 (female speaker/Caiaimage/Martin Barraud), 25 (sports team coach/SolStock), 45 (employee leaving work/Hero Images), 51 (woman looking at notes/PeopleImages), 54 (Quinceañera/Pixelchrome Inc), 55 (women in laundromat/Hero Images), 72 (graduates/© Hiya Images/Corbis), 77 (man moving house/Matthias Ritzmann), 87 (circuit board/TimeStopper), 88 (Gordon Moore/Justin Sullivan), 89 (tech items/Yuri_Arcurs), 94 (solar windows/Ashley Cooper), 101 (engineers working on turbines/Westend61), 102 (man spraying crops/D-Keine), 107 (farmer with tablet/Ariel Skelley), 117 (scientists monitoring bananas/chinaface), 123 (fat chicken/Suphanat Wongsanuphat), 125 (underwater grown tomatoes/Alexis Rosenfeld), 126 (winter climbers /David Trood), 129 (colleagues chatting in office/Ezra Bailey), 130 (Scott Nash/The Washington Post), (John Paul DeJoria/John M. Heller), (Michael Acton Smith/Oli Scarff/Staff), 132 (woman looking at whiteboard/andresr), 134 (man and woman reviewing CVs/Hero Images), 136 (woman delivering drinks/Paul Bradbury), 137 (woman in office/electravk), 139 (interns at tech company/Anchiy), 141 (women shaking hands/laflor), 143 (friends in café/ferrantraite), 145 (hand petting rhino/Suneet Bhardwaj), (woman walking down steps/gradyreese), 151 (committee job interview/filadendron), 162 (twin babies/YinYang), 178 (miniature drone/Andre Dancer/EyeEm), 193 (car engineer/Monty Rakusen), 201 (woman hugging robot/NurPhoto), (medical care robot/JIJI PRESS/Stringer); **OUP:** p. 35 (smiling woman); **Shutterstock:** pp. 14 (employee at door/Dean Drobot), 26 (modern workplace/JVHEPhoto), 28 (tidy work desk/thodonal88), 35 (colorful ties/Fedor Selivanov), 36 (McDonalds sign/Jonathan Weiss), (Tiffany box/AlesiaKan), (Easyjet airplane/NUI BLANCO), (NYC taxi/elbud), (Apple logo/r.classen), (Starbucks logo/CHALERMPHON SRISANG), (Louboutin shoes/andersphoto), 37 (pink insulation in house/Rachid Jalayanadeja), 40 (waterfront promenade/Malgorzata Litkowska), 41 (messy work desk/Andrey_Popov), 46 (casually dressed man/Rido), (formal dressed man/Bangkok Click Studio), 57 (teacher/Monkey Business Images), 60 (man thinking/Syda Productions), 64 (friends laughing/Monkey Business Images), 66 (laptop/LightField Studios), 84 (waterwheel/nikolansfoto), 110 (large plate of fries/stockcreations), 112 (chocolates/Iakov Filimonov), 114 (ice cream sundae/stockcreations), 119 (strawberry ice cream/beats1), 122 (men in café/Sjale), 123 (ripe raspberries/Olexandr Panchenko), (moldy raspberries/Andrzej Rostek), (slim chicken/Jakkrit Phomwong), 156 (cookies/Mouse family), (rechargeable batteries/art_photo_sib), (tea/Arancio), 159 (lightbulb moment/Billion Photos), 161 (prehistoric cave paintings/thipjang), 174 (Rosetta Stone/Claudio Divizia), 180 (factory with robots/AlexLMX), (self-checkout/frantic00), (robot vacuum cleaner/Jtal), (robot arm/THINK A), 183 (pilots in cockpit/Skycolors), 184 (automation concept/PopTika), 187 (adult photographing scenery/ProStockStudio), 188 (driverless car/Snapic_PhotoProduction), 191 (smart home/zhu difeng), 193 (dentist and patient/Africa Studio), (dietician/Stasique), 194 (self-driving truck/Tony Avelar/AP), 195 (3D printer/science photo), 198 (robot typing on computer/Andrey_Popov), 200 (woman talking on phone/Antonio Guillem); **Third party:** pp. 30 (Leon Heppel/Office of NIH History and Stetten Museum, U.S. National Institutes of Health), 57 (Rachel Weinstein/Rachel Weinstein/Adulting school), 80 (Hannah Herbst/Julie Herbst).

ACKNOWLEDGMENTS

We would like to acknowledge the teachers from all over the world who participated in the development process and review of *Q: Skills for Success* Third Edition.

USA

Kate Austin, Avila University, MO; **Sydney Bassett**, Auburn Global University, AL; **Michael Beamer**, USC, CA; **Renae Betten**, CBU, CA; **Pepper Boyer**, Auburn Global University, AL; **Marina Broeder**, Mission College, CA; **Thomas Brynmore**, Auburn Global University, AL; **Britta Burton**, Mission College, CA; **Kathleen Castello**, Mission College, CA; **Teresa Cheung**, North Shore Community College, MA; **Shantall Colebrooke**, Auburn Global University, AL; **Kyle Cooper**, Troy University, AL; **Elizabeth Cox**, Auburn Global University, AL; **Ashley Ekers**, Auburn Global University, AL; **Rhonda Farley**, Los Rios Community College, CA; **Marcus Frame**, Troy University, AL; **Lora Glaser**, Mission College, CA; **Hala Hamka**, Henry Ford College, MI; **Shelley A. Harrington**, Henry Ford College, MI; **Barrett J. Heusch**, Troy University, AL; **Beth Hill**, St. Charles Community College, MO; **Patty Jones**, Troy University, AL; **Tom Justice**, North Shore Community College, MA; **Robert Klein**, Troy University, AL; **Patrick Maestas**, Auburn Global University, AL; **Elizabeth Merchant**, Auburn Global University, AL; **Rosemary Miketa**, Henry Ford College, MI; **Myo Myint**, Mission College, CA; **Lance Noe**, Troy University, AL; **Irene Pannatier**, Auburn Global University, AL; **Annie Percy**, Troy University, AL; **Erin Robinson**, Troy University, AL; **Juliane Rosner**, Mission College, CA; **Mary Stevens**, North Shore Community College, MA; **Pamela Stewart**, Henry Ford College, MI; **Karen Tucker**, Georgia Tech, GA; **Loreley Wheeler**, North Shore Community College, MA; **Amanda Wilcox**, Auburn Global University, AL; **Heike Williams**, Auburn Global University, AL

Canada

Angelika Brunel, Collège Ahuntsic, QC; **David Butler**, English Language Institute, BC; **Paul Edwards**, Kwantlen Polytechnic University, BC; **Cody Hawver**, University of British Columbia, BC; **Olivera Jovovic**, Kwantlen Polytechnic University, BC; **Tami Moffatt**, University of British Columbia, BC; **Dana Pynn**, Vancouver Island University, BC

Latin America

Georgette Barreda, SENATI, Peru; **Claudia Cecilia Díaz Romero**, Colegio América, Mexico; **Jeferson Ferro**, Uninter, Brazil; **Mayda Hernández**, English Center, Mexico; **Jose Ixtaccihuasatl**, Instituto Tecnológico de Tecomatlán, Mexico; **Andreas Paulus Pabst**, CBA Idiomas, Brazil; **Amanda Carla Pas**, Instituição de Ensino Santa Izildinha, Brazil; **Allen Quesada Pacheco**, University of Costa Rica, Costa Rica; **Rolando Sánchez**, Escuela Normal de Tecámac, Mexico; **Luis Vasquez**, CESNO, Mexico

Asia

Asami Atsuko, Jissen Women's University, Japan; **Rene Bouchard**, Chinzei Keiai Gakuen, Japan; **Francis Brannen**, Sangmyung University, South Korea; **Haeyun Cho**, Sogang University, South Korea; **Daniel Craig**, Sangmyung University, South Korea; **Thomas Cuming**, Royal Melbourne Institute of Technology, Vietnam; **Nguyen Duc Dat**, OISP, Vietnam; **Wayne Devitte**, Tokai University, Japan; **James D. Dunn**, Tokai University, Japan; **Fergus Hann**, Tokai University, Japan; **Michael Hood**, Nihon University College of Commerce, Japan; **Hideyuki Kashimoto**, Shijonawate High School, Japan; **David Kennedy**, Nihon University, Japan; **Anna Youngna Kim**, Sogang University, South Korea; **Jae Phil Kim**, Sogang University, South Korea; **Jaganathan Krishnasamy**, GB Academy, Malaysia; **Peter Laver**, Incheon National University, South Korea; **Hung Hoang Le**, Ho Chi Minh City University of Technology, Vietnam; **Hyon Sook Lee**, Sogang University, South Korea; **Ji-seon Lee**, Iruda English Institute, South Korea; **Joo Young Lee**, Sogang University, South Korea; **Phung Tu Luc**, Ho Chi Minh City University of Technology, Vietnam; **Richard Mansbridge**, Hoa Sen University, Vietnam; **Kahoko Matsumoto**, Tokai University, Japan; **Elizabeth May**, Sangmyung University, South Korea; **Naoyuki Naganuma**, Tokai University, Japan; **Hiroko Nishikage**, Taisho University, Japan; **Yongjun Park**, Sangji University, South Korea; **Paul Rogers**, Dongguk University, South Korea; **Scott Schafer**, Inha University, South Korea; **Michael Schvaudner**, Tokai University, Japan; **Brendan Smith**, RMIT University, School of Languages and English, Vietnam; **Peter Snashall**, Huachiew Chalermprakiet University, Thailand; **Makoto Takeda**, Sendai Third Senior High School, Japan; **Peter Talley**, Mahidol University, Faculty of ICT, Thailand; **Byron Thigpen**, Sogang University, South Korea; **Junko Yamaai**, Tokai University, Japan; **Junji Yamada**, Taisho University, Japan; **Sayoko Yamashita**, Jissen Women's University, Japan; **Masami Yukimori**, Taisho University, Japan

Middle East and North Africa

Sajjad Ahmad, Taibah University, Saudi Arabia; **Basma Alansari**, Taibah University, Saudi Arabia; **Marwa Al-ashqar**, Taibah University, Saudi Arabia; **Dr. Rashid Al-Khawaldeh**, Taibah University, Saudi Arabia; **Mohamed Almohamed**, Taibah University, Saudi Arabia; **Dr Musaad Alrahaili**, Taibah University, Saudi Arabia; **Hala Al Sammar**, Kuwait University, Kuwait; **Ahmed Alshammari**, Taibah University, Saudi Arabia; **Ahmed Alshamy**, Taibah University, Saudi Arabia; **Doniazad sultan AlShraideh**, Taibah University, Saudi Arabia; **Sahar Amer**, Taibah University, Saudi Arabia; **Nabeela Azam**, Taibah University, Saudi Arabia; **Hassan Bashir**, Edex, Saudi Arabia; **Rachel Batchilder**, College of the North Atlantic, Qatar; **Nicole Cuddie**, Community College of Qatar, Qatar; **Mahdi Duris**, King Saud University, Saudi Arabia; **Ahmed Ege**, Institute of Public Administration, Saudi Arabia; **Magda Fadle**, Victoria College, Egypt; **Mohammed Hassan**, Taibah University, Saudi Arabia; **Tom Hodgson**, Community College of Qatar, Qatar; **Ayub Agbar Khan**, Taibah University, Saudi Arabia; **Cynthia Le Joncour**, Taibah University, Saudi Arabia; **Ruari Alexander MacLeod**, Community College of Qatar, Qatar; **Nasir Mahmood**, Taibah University, Saudi Arabia; **Duria Salih Mahmoud**, Taibah University, Saudi Arabia; **Ameera McKoy**, Taibah University, Saudi Arabia; **Chaker Mhamdi**, Buraimi University College, Oman; **Baraa Shiekh Mohamed**, Community College of Qatar, Qatar; **Abduleelah Mohammed**, Taibah University, Saudi Arabia; **Shumaila Nasir**, Taibah University, Saudi Arabia; **Kevin Onwordi**, Taibah University, Saudi Arabia; **Dr. Navid Rahmani**, Community College of Qatar, Qatar; **Dr. Sabah Salman Sabbah**, Community College of Qatar, Qatar; **Salih**, Taibah University, Saudi Arabia; **Verna Santos-Nafrada**, King Saud University, Saudi Arabia; **Gamal Abdelfattah Shehata**, Taibah University, Saudi Arabia; **Ron Stefan**, Institute of Public Administration, Saudi Arabia; **Dr. Saad Torki**, Imam Abdulrahman Bin Faisal University, Dammam, Saudi Arabia; **Silvia Yafai**, Applied Technology High School/Secondary Technical School, UAE; **Mahmood Zar**, Taibah University, Saudi Arabia; **Thouraya Zheni**, Taibah University, Saudi Arabia

Turkey

Sema Babacan, Istanbul Medipol University; **Bilge Çöllüoğlu Yakar**, Bilkent University; **Liana Corniel**, Koc University; **Savas Geylanioglu**, Izmir Bahcesehir Science and Technology College; **Öznur Güler**, Giresun University; **Selen Bilginer Halefoğlu**, Maltepe University; **Ahmet Konukoğlu**, Hasan Kalyoncu University; **Mehmet Salih Yoğun**, Gaziantep Hasan Kalyoncu University; **Fatih Yücel**, Beykent University

Europe

Irina Gerasimova, Saint-Petersburg Mining University, Russia; **Amina Al Hashamia**, University of Exeter, UK; **Jodi**, Las Dominicas, Spain; **Marina Khanykova**, School 179, Russia; **Oksana Postnikova**, Lingua Practica, Russia; **Nina Vasilchenko**, Soho-Bridge Language School, Russia

Q: Skills for Success THIRD EDITION

CRITICAL THINKING

The unique critical thinking approach of the *Q: Skills for Success* series has been further enhanced in the Third Edition. New features help you analyze, synthesize, and develop your ideas.

Unit question
The thought-provoking unit questions engage you with the topic and provide a critical thinking framework for the unit.

UNIT QUESTION
What makes a good leader?

A. Discuss these questions with your classmates.
1. Have you ever been a leader? For example, have you ever been in charge of a group at school or been the captain of a sports team? If so, what challenges did you face as a leader?
2. Think of a leader you admire. What makes this person a good leader?

Analysis
You can discuss your opinion of each listening text and analyze how it changes your perspective on the unit question.

SAY WHAT YOU THINK

SYNTHESIZE Think about Listening 1, Listening 2, and the unit video as you discuss the questions.

1. The speakers suggest that the appearance of a product or a space can send a message. What message do you send by your own appearance and the appearance of your possessions?
2. Think about a time that you judged someone based on how he or she looked or organized things. Was your first impression right or wrong? Why?
3. How can colors help a person to be more organized? How could a productive messy person use color to find things more easily?

NEW! Critical Thinking Strategy with video
Each unit includes a Critical Thinking Strategy with activities to give you step-by-step guidance in critical analysis of texts. An accompanying instructional video (available on iQ Online) provides extra support and examples.

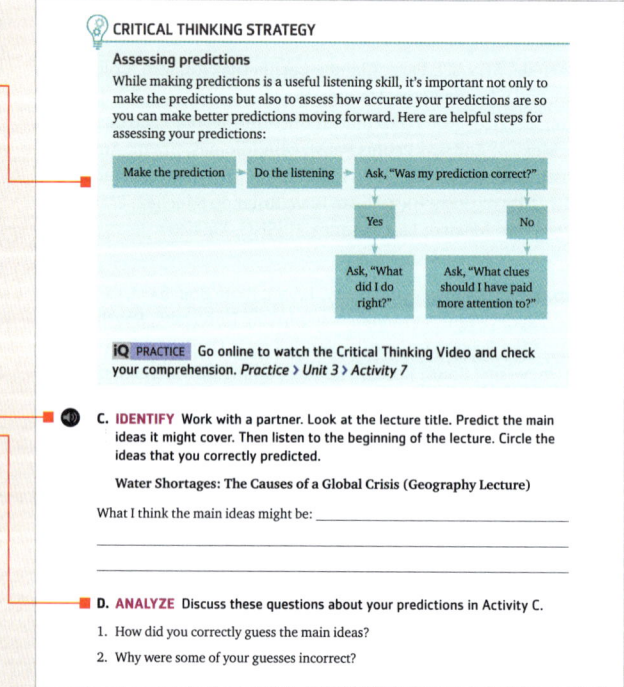

CRITICAL THINKING STRATEGY

Assessing predictions
While making predictions is a useful listening skill, it's important not only to make the predictions but also to assess how accurate your predictions are so you can make better predictions moving forward. Here are helpful steps for assessing your predictions:

Make the prediction → Do the listening → Ask, "Was my prediction correct?"
- Yes → Ask, "What did I do right?"
- No → Ask, "What clues should I have paid more attention to?"

iQ PRACTICE Go online to watch the Critical Thinking Video and check your comprehension. *Practice > Unit 3 > Activity 7*

C. **IDENTIFY** Work with a partner. Look at the lecture title. Predict the main ideas it might cover. Then listen to the beginning of the lecture. Circle the ideas that you correctly predicted.

Water Shortages: The Causes of a Global Crisis (Geography Lecture)

What I think the main ideas might be: _____
_____
_____

D. **ANALYZE** Discuss these questions about your predictions in Activity C.
1. How did you correctly guess the main ideas?
2. Why were some of your guesses incorrect?

NEW! Bloom's Taxonomy
Pink activity headings integrate verbs from Bloom's Taxonomy to help you see how each activity develops critical thinking skills.

THREE TYPES OF VIDEO

UNIT VIDEO

The unit videos include high-interest documentaries and reports on a wide variety of subjects, all linked to the unit topic and question.

NEW! "Work with the Video" pages guide you in watching, understanding, and discussing the unit videos. The activities help you see the connection to the Unit Question and the other texts in the unit.

NEW! In some units, one of the main listening texts is a video.

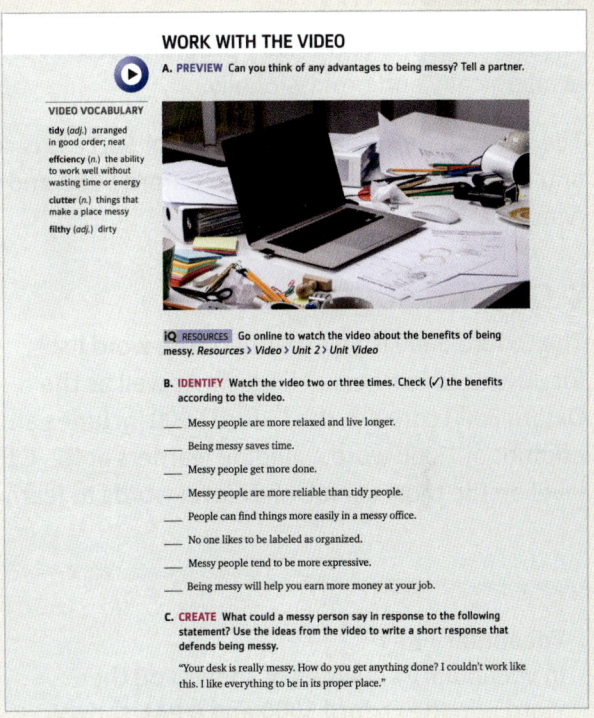

CRITICAL THINKING VIDEO

NEW! Narrated by the *Q* series authors, these short videos give you further instruction on the Critical Thinking Strategy of each unit using engaging images and graphics. You can use them to gain a deeper understanding of the Critical Thinking Strategy.

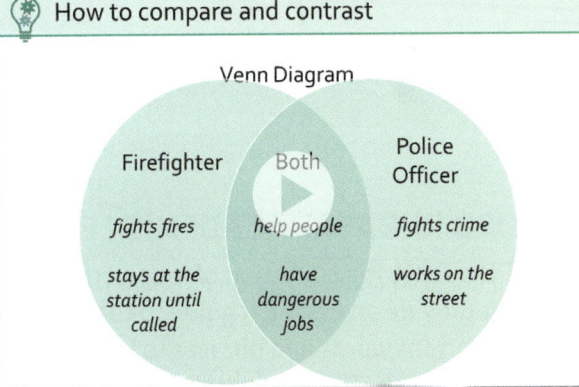

SKILLS VIDEO

NEW! These instructional videos provide illustrated explanations of skills and grammar points in the Student Book. They can be viewed in class or assigned for a flipped classroom, for homework, or for review. One skill video is available for every unit.

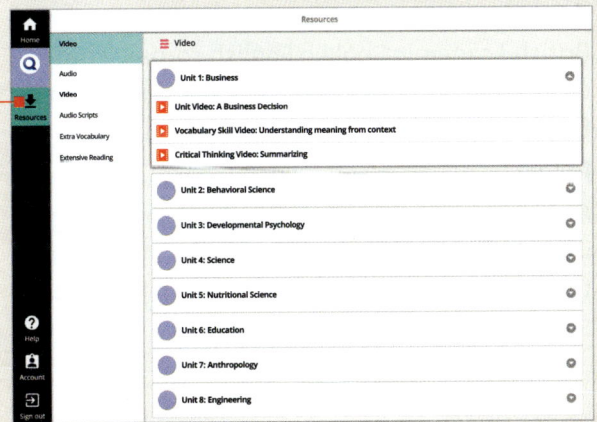

Easily access all videos in the Resources section of iQ Online.

VOCABULARY

A research-based vocabulary program focuses on the words you need to know academically and professionally.

The vocabulary syllabus in *Q: Skills for Success* is correlated to the CEFR (see page 102) and linked to two word lists: the Oxford 5000 and the OPAL (Oxford Phrasal Academic Lexicon).

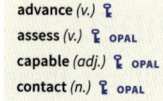 OXFORD 5000

The Oxford 5000 is an expanded core word list for advanced learners of English. As well as the Oxford 3000 core list, the Oxford 5000 includes an additional 2,000 words, guiding learners at B2–C1 level on the most useful, high-level words to learn.

> **PREVIEW THE LISTENING**
>
> **A. PREVIEW** In this lecture, the speaker presents some of the negative ways in which successful executives may change. What are two ways you think people tend to change negatively when they become leaders?
>
> **B. VOCABULARY** Read aloud these words from Listening 2. Check (✓) the ones you know. Use a dictionary to define any new or unknown words. Then discuss with a partner how the words will relate to the unit.
>
> | advance (v.) | effective (adj.) OPAL | style (n.) OPAL |
> | assess (v.) OPAL | ethical (adj.) OPAL | title (n.) OPAL |
> | capable (adj.) OPAL | executive (n.) | |
> | contact (n.) OPAL | perspective (n.) OPAL | |
>
> Oxford 5000™ words   OPAL Oxford Phrasal Academic Lexicon
>
> **iQ PRACTICE** Go online to listen and practice your pronunciation.
> Practice > Unit 1 > Activity 7

Vocabulary Key
In vocabulary activities, shows you the word is in the Oxford 5000 and **OPAL** shows you the word or phrase is in the OPAL.

OPAL
OXFORD PHRASAL ACADEMIC LEXICON

NEW! The OPAL is a collection of four word lists that provide an essential guide to the most important words and phrases to know for academic English. The word lists are based on the Oxford Corpus of Academic English and the British Academic Spoken English corpus. The OPAL includes both spoken and written academic English and both individual words and longer phrases.

Academic Language tips in the Student Book give information about how words and phrases from the OPAL are used and offer help with features such as collocations and phrases.

> **CATEGORIZE** Read and listen to the presentation about happy appearance. Complete the notes in the T-chart
>
> **ACADEMIC LANGUAGE**
> It's helpful to listen for key phrases that communicate a contrast. Phrases like *on the other hand*, *at the same time*, *rather than*, and *but in fact* tell the listener that contrasting information is coming up.
>
> OPAL
> Oxford Phrasal Academic Lexicon
>
> Sure, we all look better when we smile, but can ou really cause us to succeed or fail? Many scientists bel lead to more success in life, while frowning can lead Some researchers discovered that people who smiled were more likely to have longer, happier marriages i those who did not. In contrast, people who didn't sm photos tended to get divorced more often. Also, peop interviews were more likely to get the jobs than cand smile. Smiling also reduces stress, some scientists say smiling while doing a stressful job helped workers' br recover from the stress more quickly afterward. On t who didn't smile had faster heartbeats long after the job. Maybe this is why smiling can even cause people research study discovered that if baseball players wer cards, they lived almost seven years longer than play smiling. So remember to smile!

EXTENSIVE READING

NEW! Extensive Reading is a program of reading for pleasure at a level that matches your language ability.

There are many benefits to Extensive Reading:
- It helps you to become a better reader in general.
- It helps to increase your reading speed.
- It can improve your reading comprehension.
- It increases your vocabulary range.
- It can help you improve your grammar and writing skills.
- It's great for motivation to read something that is interesting for its own sake.

Each unit of *Q: Skills for Success* Third Edition has been aligned to an Oxford Graded Reader based on the appropriate topic and level of language proficiency. The first chapter of each recommended graded reader can be downloaded from iQ Online Resources.

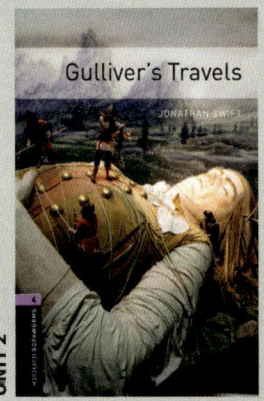
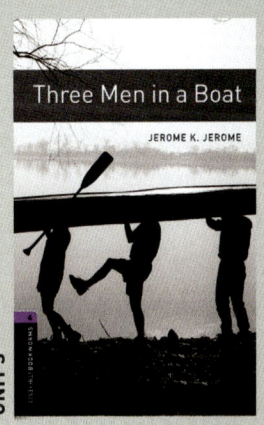

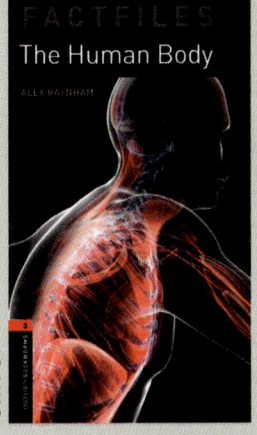
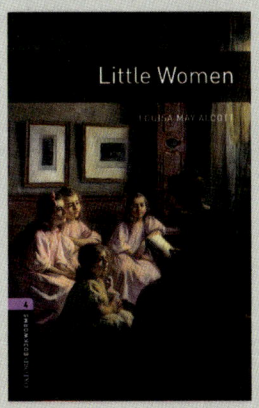

What is iQ ONLINE?

iQ ONLINE extends your learning beyond the classroom.

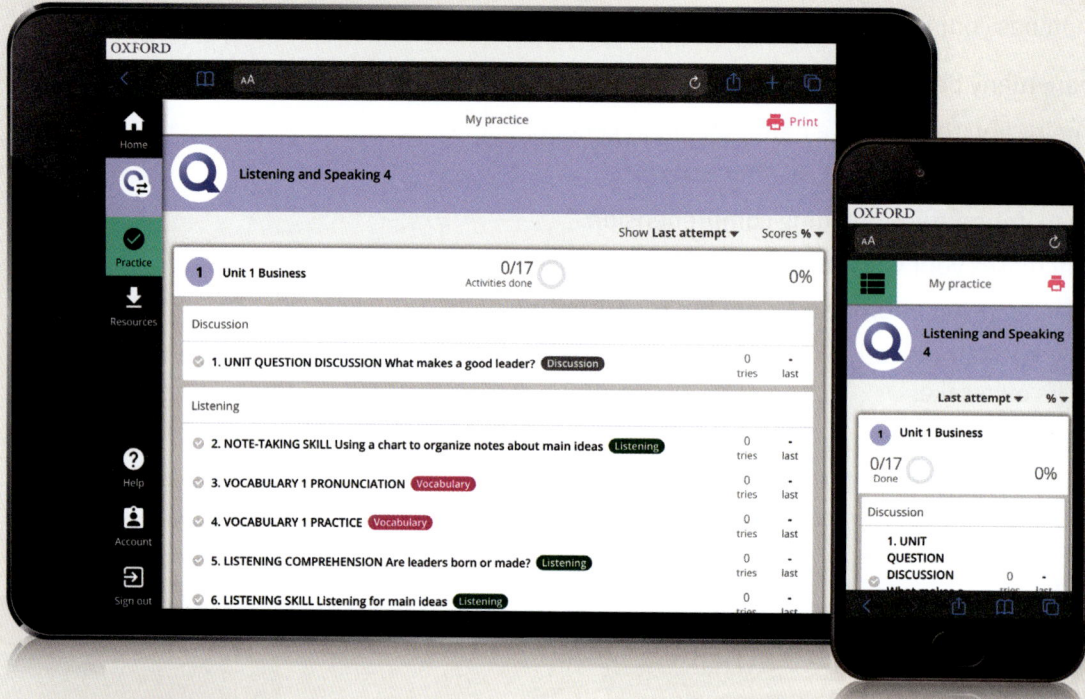

- Practice activities provide essential skills practice and support.
- Automatic grading and progress reports show you what you have mastered and where you need more practice.
- The Discussion Board allows you to discuss the Unit Questions and helps you develop your critical thinking.
- Essential resources such as audio and video are easy to access anytime.

NEW TO THE THIRD EDITION

- iQ Online is optimized for mobile use so you can use it on your phone.
- An updated interface allows easy navigation around the activities, tests, resources, and scores.
- New Critical Thinking Videos expand on the Critical Thinking Strategies in the Student Book.
- The Extensive Reading program helps you improve your vocabulary and reading skills.

go.oup.com/hub

How to use iQ ONLINE

Go to **Practice** to find additional practice and support to complement your learning in the classroom.

Go to **Resources** to find:
- All Student Book video
- All Student Book audio
- Critical Thinking videos
- Skills videos
- Extensive Reading

Go to **Messages** and **Discussion Board** to communicate with your teacher and classmates.

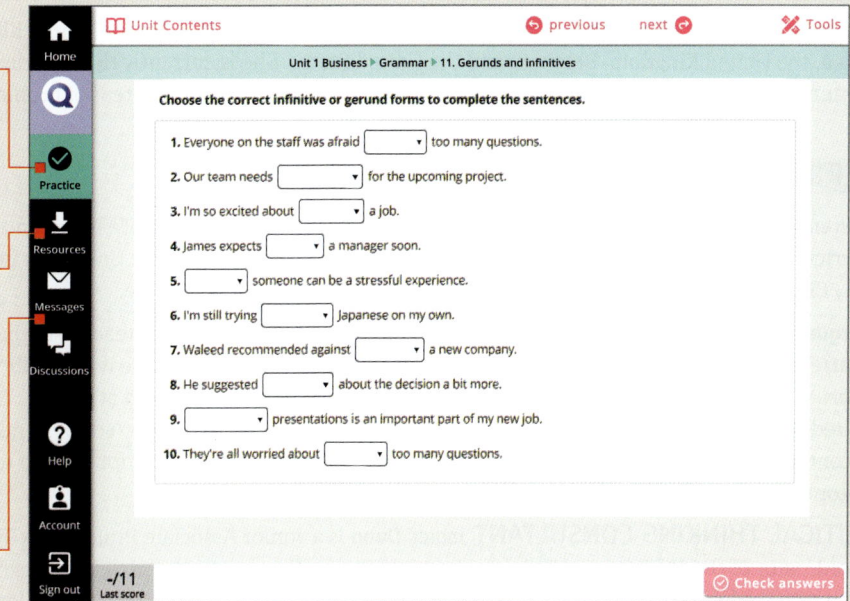

A progress bar shows you how many activities you have completed.

View your scores for all activities.

Online tests assigned by your teacher help you assess your progress and see where you need more practice.

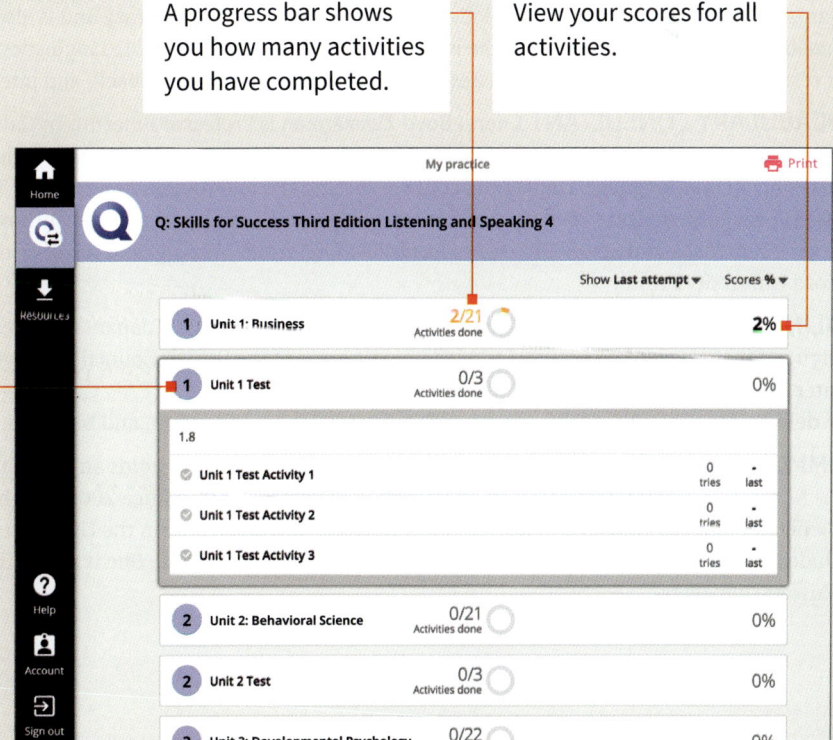

AUTHORS AND CONSULTANTS

AUTHORS

Robert Freire holds an M.A. in Applied Linguistics from Montclair State University in New Jersey. He is a teacher and materials developer with more than ten years of ELT experience. He most recently taught ESL and linguistics at Montclair State University.

Tamara Jones holds a Ph.D. in Education from the University of Sheffield in the United Kingdom. She has taught in Russia, Korea, the United Kingdom, Belgium, and the United States. She is currently the Associate Director of the English Language Center at Howard Community College in Maryland. She specializes in the areas of pronunciation and conversation.

SERIES CONSULTANTS

Lawrence J. Zwier holds an M.A. in TESL from the University of Minnesota. He is currently the Associate Director for Curriculum Development at the English Language Center at Michigan State University in East Lansing. He has taught ESL/EFL in the United States, Saudi Arabia, Malaysia, Japan, and Singapore.

Marguerite Ann Snow holds a Ph.D. in Applied Linguistics from UCLA. She teaches in the TESOL M.A. program in the Charter College of Education at California State University, Los Angeles. She was a Fulbright scholar in Hong Kong and Cyprus. In 2006, she received the President's Distinguished Professor award at CSULA. She has trained ESL teachers in the United States and EFL teachers in more than 25 countries. She is the author/editor of numerous publications in the areas of content-based instruction, English for academic purposes, and standards for English teaching and learning. She is a co-editor of *Teaching English as a Second or Foreign Language* (4th ed.).

CRITICAL THINKING CONSULTANT James Dunn is a Junior Associate Professor at Tokai University and the Coordinator of the JALT Critical Thinking Special Interest Group. His research interests include critical thinking skills' impact on student brain function during English learning as measured by EEG. His educational goals are to help students understand that they are capable of more than they might think and to expand their cultural competence with critical thinking and higher-order thinking skills.

ASSESSMENT CONSULTANT Elaine Boyd has worked in assessment for over 30 years for international testing organizations. She has designed and delivered courses in assessment literacy and is also the author of several EL exam coursebooks for leading publishers. She is an Associate Tutor (M.A. TESOL/Linguistics) at University College, London. Her research interests are classroom assessment, issues in managing feedback, and intercultural competences.

VOCABULARY CONSULTANT Cheryl Boyd Zimmerman is Professor Emeritus at California State University, Fullerton. She specialized in second-language vocabulary acquisition, an area in which she is widely published. She taught graduate courses on second-language acquisition, culture, vocabulary, and the fundamentals of TESOL, and has been a frequent invited speaker on topics related to vocabulary teaching and learning. She is the author of *Word Knowledge: A Vocabulary Teacher's Handbook* and Series Director of *Inside Reading, Inside Writing*, and *Inside Listening and Speaking*, published by Oxford University Press.

ONLINE INTEGRATION Chantal Hemmi holds an Ed.D. TEFL and is a Japan-based teacher trainer and curriculum designer. Since leaving her position as Academic Director of the British Council in Tokyo, she has been teaching at the Center for Language Education and Research at Sophia University in an EAP/CLIL program offered for undergraduates. She delivers lectures and teacher trainings throughout Japan, Indonesia, and Malaysia.

COMMUNICATIVE GRAMMAR CONSULTANT Nancy Schoenfeld holds an M.A. in TESOL from Biola University in La Mirada, California, and has been an English language instructor since 2000. She has taught ESL in California and Hawaii, and EFL in Thailand and Kuwait. She has also trained teachers in the United States and Indonesia. Her interests include teaching vocabulary, extensive reading, and student motivation. She is currently an English Language Instructor at Kuwait University.

CONTENTS

Welcome to *Q: Skills for Success* Third Edition iv
What is iQ Online? viii
Authors and Consultants x

UNIT 1 Business – What makes a good leader? **2**
    Note-taking Skill: Using a chart to organize notes about main ideas 4
    Listening 1: Leadership Isn't Just for the Boss 5
    Listening Skill: Listening for main ideas 9
    Listening 2: Myths of Effective Leadership 11
    Work with the Video: A Business Decision 16
    Vocabulary Skill: Understanding meaning from context 17
    Grammar: Gerunds and infinitives 19
    Pronunciation: Syllable stress 21
    Critical Thinking Strategy: Summarizing 21
    Speaking Skill: Checking for understanding 22
    Unit Assignment: Give a presentation on how to be an effective leader 22

UNIT 2 Behavioral Science – How does appearance affect our success? **26**
    Listening 1: A Perfect Mess 28
    Listening Skill: Identifying details 33
    Note-taking Skill: Taking notes to compare and contrast 34
    Listening 2: Color Schemes: How Colors Make You Buy 35
    Work with the Video: Benefits to Being Messy 41
    Vocabulary Skill: Using the dictionary: words with multiple definitions 42
    Grammar: Subjunctive for suggestions 44
    Pronunciation: Unstressed syllables 46
    Critical Thinking Strategy: Restating information 47
    Speaking Skill: Confirming understanding 48
    Unit Assignment: Role-play a conversation 49

UNIT 3 Developmental Psychology – What skills make someone an adult? **52**
    Note-taking Skill: Taking notes using key words and phrases 54
    Listening 1 (Video): "Adulting" School 55
    Listening Skill: Making predictions 59
    Critical Thinking Strategy: Assessing predictions 61
    Listening 2: Financial Literacy Among Young People 62
    Vocabulary Skill: Using the dictionary: words with similar meanings 67
    Grammar: Phrasal verbs 69
    Pronunciation: Sentence stress 71
    Speaking Skill: Giving a presentation 72
    Unit Assignment: Give a presentation to a group 74

UNIT 4 Science – How do the laws of science affect our lives? **78**
    Note-taking Skill: Using a split page 80
    Listening 1: Gravity at Work 81
    Listening Skill: Making inferences 85
    Listening 2 (Video): Moore's Law 87
    Vocabulary Skill: Word forms 91
    Critical Thinking Strategy: Distinguishing between similar words 92
    Grammar: Present perfect and present perfect continuous 93
    Pronunciation: Basic intonation patterns 95
    Speaking Skill: Avoiding answering questions 97
    Unit Assignment: Present a business plan 98

Vocabulary List and CEFR Correlation 102

Business 1

NOTE-TAKING	using a chart to organize notes about main ideas
LISTENING	listening for main ideas
VOCABULARY	understanding meaning from context
GRAMMAR	gerunds and infinitives
PRONUNCIATION	syllable stress
CRITICAL THINKING	summarizing
SPEAKING	checking for understanding

 **UNIT QUESTION**

What makes a good leader?

A. Discuss these questions with your classmates.

1. Have you ever been a leader? For example, have you ever been in charge of a group at school or been the captain of a sports team? If so, what challenges did you face as a leader?

2. Think of a leader you admire. What makes this person a good leader?

3. Look at the photo. Identify the leader. What qualities might make this person an effective leader?

B. Listen to *The Q Classroom* online. Then answer these questions.

1. Yuna feels that leaders should act more responsibly when they have power. Do you agree? Why or why not?

2. Felix says that becoming a leader makes a person's life difficult in some ways. Do you agree? If so, in what ways do you think becoming a leader would make a person's life difficult?

iQ PRACTICE Go to the online discussion board to discuss the Unit Question with your classmates. *Practice > Unit 1 > Activity 1*

UNIT OBJECTIVE

Listen to a radio interview and a lecture and gather information and ideas to give a presentation about how to be an effective leader.

NOTE-TAKING SKILL Using a chart to organize notes about main ideas

Charts are a useful way to organize your notes on a presentation. Using a chart to list main ideas can help you understand how a presentation is organized and can help you identify the speaker's most important points.

To organize your notes about main ideas, divide your page into two columns. Use the left column to show how the presentation is organized. Use the right column to write down the main ideas. You can also write any key words or phrases that support each main idea.

Look at the example below from Activity A. The student uses the left column to show the topics in a text and the right column to show the main ideas and key phrases.

Topic: Motivating teams	Main ideas and key phrases
First way	Make expectations clear
	- gives team a goal

A. IDENTIFY Listen to part of a talk about motivating team members. Note the main ideas in the chart.

Topic: Motivating teams	Main ideas and key phrases
First way	Make expectations clear — gives team a goal —
Second way	
Third way	

B. APPLY Listen again. In the chart, add key words and phrases that support each main idea. Compare your notes with a partner. Then take turns coming up with your own examples of each way to motivate team members.

iQ PRACTICE Go online for more practice using a chart to organize notes about main ideas. *Practice > Unit 1 > Activity 2*

LISTENING

LISTENING 1

Leadership Isn't Just for the Boss

OBJECTIVE ▶

You are going to listen to a radio interview from the Canadian Broadcasting Company about leadership at all levels of an organization. As you listen to the conversation, gather information and ideas about leadership qualities and how organizations can create leadership opportunities across their workforce.

PREVIEW THE LISTENING

A. PREVIEW Before you listen, discuss the questions in a small group.

1. What are some important leadership qualities? What adjectives describe good leaders?

2. Former American president John Quincy Adams said, "If your actions inspire others to dream more, learn more, do more, and become more, you are a leader." What do you think this quote means? Do you agree?

B. VOCABULARY Read aloud these words from Listening 1. Check (✓) the ones you know. Use a dictionary to define any new or unknown words. Then discuss with a partner how the words will relate to the unit.

clarity (n.) 🔑	motivation (n.) 🔑 OPAL	role (n.) 🔑 OPAL
enthusiasm (n.) 🔑	promote (v.) 🔑 OPAL	take on (v. phr.) 🔑
initiative (n.) 🔑 OPAL	realistic (adj.) 🔑	versus (prep.) 🔑 OPAL
innovation (n.) 🔑	responsibility (n.) 🔑 OPAL	

🔑 Oxford 5000™ words   OPAL Oxford Phrasal Academic Lexicon

iQ PRACTICE Go online to listen and practice your pronunciation.
Practice > Unit 1 > Activity 3

WORK WITH THE LISTENING

 A. LISTEN AND TAKE NOTES Listen to the radio interview and take notes on the speaker's central ideas and suggestions. Write the main ideas and key phrases you hear.

iQ RESOURCES Go online to download extra vocabulary support.
Resources > Extra Vocabulary > Unit 1

Leadership topics	Main ideas and key phrases
Important leadership qualities	
What organizations can do to encourage leadership at all levels	
Benefits to having leadership at all levels	

B. CATEGORIZE Read the statements. Write *T* (true) or *F* (false). Then correct each false statement to make it true.

___ 1. Effective companies put all their workers in leadership roles.

___ 2. One way companies can encourage leadership is by creating opportunities for people to work with other teams.

___ 3. A lack of clarity in organizations creates opportunities for creativity.

___ 4. Demonstrating initiative is a good way to be leader-like.

___ 5. Good leaders build relationships by leaving employees alone.

 **C. IDENTIFY** Read the sentences. Then listen again. Circle the correct answers.

1. Why is it good for a company to create opportunities for people to act more leader-like at all levels?

   a. Because having a lot of supervisors means more work gets done

   b. Because doing so promotes innovation, creativity, and motivation

   c. Because more responsibility makes workers happier

6 UNIT 1 What makes a good leader?

2. What is the benefit to having employees work outside their teams?
   a. They can form more friendships at work.
   b. They can share the work and get finished faster.
   c. They have an opportunity to try different things.
3. What do organizations have to have in order for their employees to thrive?
   a. Clear expectations and goals
   b. Enough room to have many leadership positions
   c. A fun work environment
4. How can people demonstrate initiative at work?
   a. By taking on a task without waiting for direction
   b. By telling their boss what he or she is doing wrong
   c. By coming early in the morning
5. Why should workers try to be friendly at work?
   a. Because it will make them feel happier
   b. Because their boss will want to spend time with them
   c. Because their attitude will motivate their co-workers

D. INTERPRET Read the comments below. Based on the listening, are the speakers demonstrating leader-like qualities? Write *Y* (yes) or *N* (no).

_____ 1. "When I get to work, I get right to business. After all, the company isn't paying me to chat with my co-workers."

_____ 2. "I am a low-level manager in a big company. I expect my employees to obey me because I am their boss. They don't need to know why I tell them to do things."

_____ 3. "I enjoy working on projects with other departments. It sparks my creativity when I think outside the box."

_____ 4. "I don't like to take on too much responsibility at work. It's important to me to have free time for my real interests and hobbies. Work is just a way to make money for life."

_____ 5. "I think it's important for my employees to understand my plan for the company and for them to be clear about the direction I want the company to go in."

_____ 6. "Even when I am not feeling it, I try to demonstrate my excitement to be at work. I want my employees to know that I am excited about our company. I hope they feel motivated, too."

E. CREATE Work with a partner. If you were the head of an organization, how would you make sure to hire people who demonstrated leadership qualities? Create questions that you could ask potential employees in a job interview to determine whether they are leader-like.

F. VOCABULARY Here are some words from Listening 1. Complete each sentence with the correct word.

clarity (n.)	innovation (n.)	realistic (adj.)	take on (v. phr.)
enthusiasm (n.)	motivation (n.)	responsibility (n.)	versus (prep.)
initiative (n.)	promote (v.)	role (n.)	

1. Young people are often responsible for much of the exciting _____ happening in the tech world because they often have new and fresh ideas.

2. An employee's _____ is the part that person plays in the organization.

3. Some animals _____ the colors of their environments so they can hide from predators better.

4. Many people say that money is the main _____ for working.

5. The company bought time on a TV station to _____ its new product.

6. It's not _____ to think you will ever win the lottery.

7. If you want to get ahead at work, you need to show some _____ by taking on responsibilities without being asked first.

8. Looking the word up in the dictionary gave me a lot of _____. I really feel like I understand the text better now.

9. When you are choosing a career, you need to compare the benefits of money _____ job satisfaction.

10. She does her job with such _____ that it's fun to work with her.

11. Good supervisors take _____ for their employees.

iQ PRACTICE Go online for more practice with the vocabulary.
Practice > Unit 1 > Activity 4

iQ PRACTICE Go online for additional listening and comprehension.
Practice > Unit 1 > Activity 5

SAY WHAT YOU THINK

DISCUSS Work in a group to discuss the questions.

1. The interview discussed the benefits of encouraging leader-like behavior at all levels. What are some possible disadvantages?
2. Recall the leadership qualities the speaker described in the radio interview. Share examples of times you have shown these qualities.

LISTENING SKILL Listening for main ideas

When listening to a presentation, it is difficult to remember every piece of information you hear. Instead of trying to remember every detail, it is more important to identify the speaker's **main ideas**. These are the most important ideas that the speaker wants you to understand and remember.

A speaker often states the main ideas as part of the introduction. Here are some signal phrases used to introduce main ideas.

> Today <u>we'll focus on</u> . . .
> This morning <u>we'll consider</u> . . .
> Today <u>I'm going to talk about</u> . . .
> For today's lecture, <u>we're going to look at</u> . . .

Main ideas are often repeated or rephrased during a presentation, especially at the end.

After you listen and take notes, review your notes. Notice which ideas are repeated or described in greater detail. This will help you decide what the main ideas are.

ACADEMIC LANGUAGE

In academic writing, the main ideas are often presented indirectly. However, speakers usually directly introduce their main ideas by using the future tense in phrases like *I'm going to show you* . . . , *we're going to go through* . . . , and *we're going to be talking about* . . .

―――――――― OPAL
Oxford Phrasal Academic Lexicon

 A. EVALUATE Listen to the introduction to each of three presentations. Circle the option that best describes the main idea of each introduction.

Introduction 1:
a. Meetings are often boring because they're too long and waste time.
b. Meetings are often boring, but there are ways to make them worthwhile.
c. Meetings are often boring, so we should find ways to eliminate them.

Introduction 2:
a. Job searchers should learn how to answer interview questions and write résumés.
b. Job searchers should learn how to use online job-finding tools effectively.
c. Job searchers should go online to find out about available jobs.

LISTENING 1 9

Introduction 3:

a. Many people hire employees for the wrong reasons. Soon they regret their hiring decisions.

b. It is important that managers learn to recognize that someone is not a good hiring choice.

c. Hiring employees can be difficult, but this presentation will teach skills for choosing the best possible employees.

 B. APPLY Listen to a short presentation. As you listen, take notes in the chart.

Topic	
Most important factor	
First characteristic mentioned	
Second characteristic mentioned	
Last characteristic mentioned	

iQ PRACTICE Go online for more practice listening for main ideas.
Practice > Unit 1 > Activity 6

LISTENING 2 Myths of Effective Leadership

OBJECTIVE ▶ You are going to listen to a lecture from the Center for Creative Leadership, an organization dedicated to helping executives by providing them with the information and skills they need to lead well and overcome common challenges. As you listen to the lecture, gather information and ideas about what makes a good leader.

PREVIEW THE LISTENING

A. PREVIEW In this lecture, the speaker presents some of the negative ways in which successful executives may change. What are two ways you think people tend to change negatively when they become leaders?

B. VOCABULARY Read aloud these words from Listening 2. Check (✓) the ones you know. Use a dictionary to define any new or unknown words. Then discuss with a partner how the words will relate to the unit.

advance *(v.)* 🔑	effective *(adj.)* 🔑 OPAL	style *(n.)* 🔑 OPAL
assess *(v.)* 🔑 OPAL	ethical *(adj.)* 🔑 OPAL	title *(n.)* 🔑 OPAL
capable *(adj.)* 🔑 OPAL	executive *(n.)* 🔑	
contact *(n.)* 🔑 OPAL	perspective *(n.)* 🔑 OPAL	

🔑 Oxford 5000™ words   OPAL Oxford Phrasal Academic Lexicon

iQ PRACTICE Go online to listen and practice your pronunciation.
Practice > Unit 1 > Activity 7

WORK WITH THE LISTENING

 A. LISTEN AND TAKE NOTES Listen to the lecture and take notes in the charts.

iQ RESOURCES Go online to download extra vocabulary support.
Resources > Extra Vocabulary > Unit 1

Actions of ineffective leaders	Main ideas and key phrases
First example	
Second example	
Third example	

Advice for leaders	Main ideas and key phrases
First piece of advice	
Second piece of advice	
Third piece of advice	

B. EXPLAIN Use your notes to answer the questions.

1. According to a study by the Center for Creative Leadership, how do many powerful executives see themselves?

2. What do many powerful executives think about people who disagree with them?

3. How do these employees begin to react to the executives?

C. CATEGORIZE Read the statements. Then listen again. Write *T* (true) or *F* (false). Then correct each false statement to make it true.

_____ 1. Many executives forget the skills that helped them become successful.

_____ 2. An effective executive must know the difference between power and leadership.

_____ 3. A study shows that many executives respect employees who disagree with them.

_____ 4. Many executives begin to believe they are more powerful than they really are.

_____ 5. It is impossible to learn the skills necessary for effective leadership.

_____ 6. To become an effective leader, you must view yourself through the eyes of your team members.

D. EVALUATE Read the advice on leadership. Check (✓) the advice you think the speaker would agree with. Briefly discuss your ideas with a partner.

☐ 1. When team members disagree with you, ask some questions and take time to consider their perspectives.

☐ 2. Encourage your team members to ask questions about your decisions and plans.

☐ 3. Instead of personal meetings, announce major business decisions and plans by email or video.

☐ 4. Invite team members to fill out anonymous feedback forms about your performance and your leadership style.

☐ 5. Keep your contact with team members brief. If they have concerns or complaints, encourage them to speak with your assistant.

E. CATEGORIZE Read the examples of decisions made by leaders. Based on the information in the lecture, do they demonstrate effective or ineffective leadership? Write *E* (effective) or *I* (ineffective). Then discuss your choices with a partner.

____ 1. The president of Linear Electronics, James Yoo, hires all managers from outside his company. He doesn't believe in promoting existing team members to management positions.

____ 2. Reggie Silva, head coach of the Tower University baseball team, has breakfast with players individually each month to find out how they are doing.

____ 3. Restaurant owner Claudia Tavares placed an "idea box" near the door of her restaurant. She checks it each week for thoughts from her customers.

____ 4. Daniel Lisa was elected president of his university's engineering club. He assigned people who voted for him to all the advisory board positions.

____ 5. Edgar Molina, vice president of Trident Bank, tries to read several leadership books each year.

____ 6. Governor Patricia Landon keeps her office door open so team members can come in and talk whenever they want to.

____ 7. The head of the English Literature Department, Coleen Zhang, believes it is much more efficient to make most departmental decisions on her own. Involving others in the decision-making process takes too long.

F. DISCUSS Work in a group to discuss the questions.

1. The speaker states that leadership and power are not the same. What do you think are some differences between leadership and power?

2. According to the lecture, some successful executives begin to "blur the lines" between leadership and power. They act as if leadership and power are the same thing. Why do you think this happens?

G. VOCABULARY Here are some words from Listening 2. Complete each sentence with the correct word.

advance (v.)	contact (n.)	executive (n.)	title (n.)
assess (v.)	effective (adj.)	perspective (n.)	
capable (adj.)	ethical (adj.)	style (n.)	

1. We need to hire a more _____ office assistant. The current assistant doesn't have enough experience and isn't highly skilled.

2. My management _____ is very different from Roger's. I prefer to lead by example. He prefers to give detailed instructions to employees.

3. I'm nervous about the meeting with my manager next Monday. She is going to _____ my performance for this year.

4. Blake joined the company in 2000. Within five years he was able to _____ to the position of vice president.

5. Please tell me what you think about this design. I'm interested in hearing your _____ on it.

6. Anne knows a lot of people in our industry. She has a good business _____ at the London office who can help us.

7. I am concerned that our company is not making _____ decisions. Our factory creates more pollution and waste than it needs to.

8. We created a plan to save the company. Unfortunately, it was not as _____ as we had hoped, and the company was forced to close last month.

9. I called her *Mrs. Rodgers*, but later I learned that her _____ is actually *Doctor*.

10. Emma only recently started working for the company, but her goal is to become a(n) _____ there someday. I think she will make a good manager.

iQ PRACTICE   Go online for more practice with the vocabulary.
Practice > Unit 1 > Activity 8

WORK WITH THE VIDEO

A. PREVIEW Have you had to make any difficult decisions that affected many people? What happened?

VIDEO VOCABULARY

CEO (*n.*) chief executive officer; the person with the highest rank in a business company

gut-check moment (*idm.*) a test of one's courage, character, or determination

decline (*n.*) a continuous decrease in number, value, quality, etc., of something

viral (*adj.*) used to describe a piece of information, a video, an image, etc., that is sent rapidly over the Internet from one person to another

John Donahoe

iQ RESOURCES Go online to watch the video about a business leader who had to make some difficult decisions. *Resources > Video > Unit 1 > Unit Video*

B. CATEGORIZE Watch the video two or three times. Number the following events in chronological order.

____ Employees, sellers, investors, and the media became upset.

____ John Donahoe was appointed as the CEO of eBay.

____ John Donahoe faced the sellers at the eBay Live meeting in Chicago and clearly explained why it was the right decision.

____ John Donahoe reconsidered his decision overnight.

____ John Donahoe announced his plan for big changes to eBay.

____ John Donahoe felt personally attacked when watching online videos.

____ Sellers started to organize to try to get rid of John Donahoe.

C. DISCUSS What lessons do you think John Donahoe learned from this experience? Share your opinions with a partner.

SAY WHAT YOU THINK

SYNTHESIZE Think about Listening 1, Listening 2, and the unit video as you discuss the questions.

1. Think of a leader you have met in your work or school life. Was he or she more like the leader in Listening 1 or Listening 2? Explain.

2. Listening 1, Listening 2, and the unit video all offer advice to bosses. Which advice do you think is the most valuable? Do you disagree with any of it? Why?

VOCABULARY SKILL Understanding meaning from context

One way to figure out the meaning of a word is from the **context** of the sentence it is in. Use the words around the unknown word to help you understand the new word.

> And that night, I tossed and turned, and the next morning, I said, you know what, it's worth it.

The speaker talks about "night" and "the next morning," so you can understand that "tossing and turning" is something a person might do at night.

It also helps to consider the conversation as a whole, not just one sentence. In this conversation, the speaker is talking about a big decision he had to make that he was really stressed about. From this context, you might be able to figure out that *toss and turn* means to stay awake and think about something.

iQ RESOURCES Go online to watch the Vocabulary Skill Video.
Resources > Video > Unit 1 > Vocabulary Skill Video

A. APPLY Listen to the sentences below. Use the context to match each bold word with its definition in the box.

a. natural ability to do something
b. the conditions that affect a person's behavior and development
c. to work in the correct way
d. to find an acceptable solution to a problem
e. to show or display

____ 1. The job didn't pay very well, but I loved the office and my co-workers. It was a great **environment** to work in.

____ 2. It's impossible to **function** well when you don't get along with your co-workers. I can't work in a situation like that.

____ 3. I'm sure you can **resolve** the conflict with your co-worker if you listen to each other's opinions.

____ 4. James has great **aptitude**, but he needs more training. In a year or so, he'll probably be our best programmer.

____ 5. The members of Emily's group are experienced and talented. Besides, they **exhibit** great teamwork.

🔊 **B. IDENTIFY** Listen to excerpts from Listening 1 and Listening 2. Circle the correct answers.

1. **Distinction** probably means ____.
   a. similarity
   b. importance
   c. difference

2. **Comfort zone** probably means ____.
   a. a new or different situation
   b. a situation in which you feel secure
   c. a situation that is dangerous

3. **Be tasked with** probably means ____.
   a. be given a job
   b. be asked a question
   c. have fun at work

4. **Opposing** probably means ____.
   a. smart
   b. contrasting
   c. similar

5. **Perceive** probably means ____.
   a. view
   b. enjoy
   c. dislike

C. CREATE Choose five words from Activities A and B. Write a sentence using each word. Then take turns reading your sentences aloud to a partner.

iQ PRACTICE Go online for more practice understanding meaning from context. *Practice > Unit 1 > Activity 9*

SPEAKING

OBJECTIVE ▶ At the end of this unit, you are going to give a presentation about how to be an effective leader. As you give the presentation, you will need to check that your audience understands you.

GRAMMAR Gerunds and infinitives

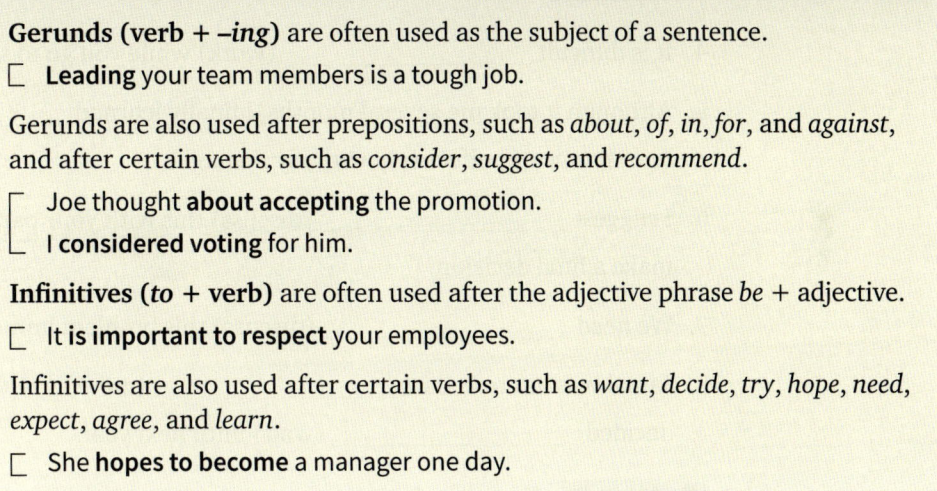

Gerunds (verb + –ing) are often used as the subject of a sentence.
- **Leading** your team members is a tough job.

Gerunds are also used after prepositions, such as *about, of, in, for,* and *against*, and after certain verbs, such as *consider, suggest,* and *recommend*.
- Joe thought **about accepting** the promotion.
- I **considered voting** for him.

Infinitives (*to* + verb) are often used after the adjective phrase *be* + adjective.
- It **is important to respect** your employees.

Infinitives are also used after certain verbs, such as *want, decide, try, hope, need, expect, agree,* and *learn*.
- She **hopes to become** a manager one day.

A. IDENTIFY Read the sentences. Underline each gerund and infinitive.

1. While every company needs a great leader, some of the most effective ones encourage their workers to take on some kind of leadership role as well.
2. What's helpful is to have leadership qualities at every level.
3. There actually is a distinction between being in a leadership role versus being a leader in your role.
4. Individuals would take initiative without waiting to get direction.
5. It gives them the opportunity to try something new.
6. So being really clear on the roles and expectations is a big thing that you can do.
7. We pay you to come to work to do your job.
8. Running a company can be a lonely, stressful experience.
9. What do you need to start a business and be successful?
10. Good leaders make people excited about being in the workplace.

B. APPLY Complete each sentence with the gerund or infinitive form of the verb in parentheses. Then practice saying the sentences with a partner.

1. Haya expects _____ (finish) business school in June.

2. This book recommends _____ (hire) people you already know.

3. _____ (work) for the government has been a great learning experience.

4. It is difficult _____ (work) while you go to school.

5. Although it took me several months, I finally learned _____ (communicate) effectively with my manager.

6. I suggest _____ (discuss) this with your partner before you make a final decision.

7. We need _____ (discuss) this problem immediately.

8. Jamal was interested in _____ (move) to Hong Kong, but he decided _____ (wait) until next year.

iQ PRACTICE Go online for more practice with gerunds and infinitives.
Practice > Unit 1 > Activities 10–11

PRONUNCIATION Syllable stress

Every word with more than one **syllable** has a syllable that is **stressed** more than the others. That stressed syllable is longer, and it has a change in pitch.

Listen to the word *negotiate*. Then repeat it.

  negotiate

The second syllable (*-go-*) is stressed. The vowel in this syllable is extra long, and it has a change in pitch.

Listen to the word again and practice saying it, stressing the second syllable.

  negotiate

Every word has its own stress pattern. Using correct word stress will make your speech clearer and easier to understand. When you learn a new word, also take note of the correct stress pattern for that word.

A. IDENTIFY Listen to the words. Which syllable is stressed? Circle each stressed syllable.

TIP FOR SUCCESS

Many dictionaries show a pronunciation guide for each entry. The pronunciation guide shows the correct syllable stress. Use a dictionary regularly to learn the stress patterns of new words.

1. (ex)cerpt
2. aspect
3. enforce
4. effective
5. leadership
6. acknowledge
7. perspective
8. opposing
9. promotion
10. interaction

B. APPLY Listen again. Then practice with a partner. Take turns saying the words.

iQ PRACTICE Go online for more practice with syllable stress.
Practice › Unit 1 › Activity 12

CRITICAL THINKING STRATEGY

Summarizing

When you **summarize**, you give a shorter version of what you heard or read, including only the main points. You should not include minor details, direct quotes, or your own opinion. Summarizing shows you understand the material.

iQ PRACTICE Go online to watch the Critical Thinking Video and check your comprehension. *Practice › Unit 1 › Activity 13*

C. COMPOSE Listen to the presentation and take notes. Work with a partner to summarize the main points.

D. DISCUSS Work in a small group. Compare your summaries and choose the most complete summary.

SPEAKING SKILL Checking for understanding

When you're giving a presentation or having a conversation, occasionally check that you are clearly communicating your ideas. To check that your listeners understand your main point(s), you can use phrases like these.

Do you know what I mean?	Are you following me?
Does that make sense?	Any questions (so far)?
Do you understand?	

A. IDENTIFY Listen to a manager giving instructions to his staff. Check (✓) the phrases he uses to check for understanding.

☐ Do you know what I mean?   ☐ Are you following me?

☐ Do you know what I'm saying?   ☐ Are you with me so far?

☐ Does that make sense?   ☐ Have you got it?

☐ Does everyone understand?   ☐ Got it?

B. RESTATE Listen again. Then work with a partner. Summarize the main points the manager wants to communicate.

iQ PRACTICE Go online for more practice checking for understanding.
Practice > Unit 1 > Activity 14

UNIT ASSIGNMENT Give a presentation on how to be an effective leader

OBJECTIVE ▶

In this assignment, you are going to give a short presentation about how to be an effective leader. As you prepare your presentation, think about the Unit Question, "What makes a good leader?" Use information from Listening 1, Listening 2, the unit video, and your work in this unit to support your presentation. Refer to the Self-Assessment checklist on page 24.

CONSIDER THE IDEAS

DISCUSS Read about a paradox, a situation that has two opposite qualities at the same time. In a group, discuss what the author means by a *power paradox*.

The Power Paradox

The best leaders understand the needs and goals of the people they lead. They are careful thinkers who understand the challenges they face. They have the ability to make intelligent choices about how to address those challenges. Great leaders are also communicators. They can explain both problems and solutions to people in a way that everyone can understand.

These abilities are not common, and when we recognize them in someone—in the business world or some other field—we are inspired to say, "That's someone I can trust! That's someone I can follow!" Unfortunately, these abilities also tend to disappear once a person actually takes on a position of leadership.

The British historian Lord Acton once said, "Power tends to corrupt, and absolute power corrupts absolutely." Researchers are now finding scientific support for Acton's claim. Many studies have shown that power can lead people to act without thinking carefully about their decisions. It can also lead people to ignore or misunderstand other people's feelings and desires.

Researchers have created experiments to see how people react when they are given power. The people who were given power over others were more likely to make risky choices, to act aggressively, to speak rudely, and to behave in ways that made others feel scared and uncomfortable. They were also more likely to tease their colleagues.

This is why we call it the *power paradox*. Power is given to people who show an ability to understand, guide, and communicate with others. But, unfortunately, once they become leaders, their power has the potential to make them rude and insensitive. In other words, what people respect and want most from leaders is often what can be damaged when someone has power.

PREPARE AND SPEAK

A. GATHER IDEAS Review the information in "The Power Paradox" about how power can affect people. Then think about the information you learned in this unit about people in positions of power. Discuss these questions with a partner.

1. What are some important skills and qualities of a leader?

2. What are negative effects that come from having power?

B. ORGANIZE IDEAS Choose two qualities and two problems from Activity A that you think are most important. Place these ideas in the first column of a chart. In a second column, list ways to develop those qualities and ways to avoid the negative effects.

C. SPEAK Present your advice to the class. As you speak, check that your classmates understand the ideas you are trying to communicate. Refer to the Self-Assessment checklist below before you begin.

iQ PRACTICE Go online for your alternate Unit Assignment.
Practice > Unit 1 > Activity 15

CHECK AND REFLECT

A. CHECK Think about the Unit Assignment as you complete the Self-Assessment checklist.

SELF-ASSESSMENT	Yes	No
I was able to speak easily about the topic.	☐	☐
My partner, group, and class understood me.	☐	☐
I understood meaning from context.	☐	☐
I used vocabulary from the unit.	☐	☐
I checked for understanding.	☐	☐
I used correct syllable stress.	☐	☐

B. REFLECT Discuss these questions with a partner or group.

1. What is something new you learned in this unit?
2. Look back at the Unit Question—What makes a good leader? Is your answer different now than when you started this unit? If yes, how is it different? Why?

iQ PRACTICE Go to the online discussion board to discuss the questions.
Practice > Unit 1 > Activity 16

TRACK YOUR SUCCESS

iQ PRACTICE Go online to check the words and phrases you have learned in this unit. *Practice > Unit 1 > Activity 17*

Check (✓) the skills and strategies you learned. If you need more work on a skill, refer to the page(s) in parentheses.

NOTE-TAKING	☐ I can use a chart to organize notes about main ideas. (p. 4)
LISTENING	☐ I can listen for main ideas. (p. 9)
VOCABULARY	☐ I can understand meaning from context. (p. 17)
GRAMMAR	☐ I can use gerunds and infinitives. (p. 19)
PRONUNCIATION	☐ I can use syllable stress. (p. 21)
CRITICAL THINKING	☐ I can summarize information. (p. 21)
SPEAKING	☐ I can check for understanding. (p. 22)
OBJECTIVE ▶	☐ I can gather information and ideas to give a presentation on how to be an effective leader.

Behavioral Science

LISTENING	identifying details
NOTE-TAKING	taking notes to compare and contrast
VOCABULARY	using the dictionary: words with multiple definitions
GRAMMAR	subjunctive for suggestions
PRONUNCIATION	unstressed syllables
CRITICAL THINKING	restating information
SPEAKING	confirming understanding

 **UNIT QUESTION**

How does appearance affect our success?

A. Discuss these questions with your classmates.

1. Think about a product you recently bought. How did the appearance (color, shape, size) affect your decision to buy it?

2. Do you think people who are organized are also more likely to be successful? How might appearing organized make someone seem successful?

3. Look at the photo. What does this workspace tell you about the people who work here? Would you like to work in a space like this? Why or why not?

B. Listen to *The Q Classroom* online. Then answer these questions.

1. Sophy believes that how we dress affects what people think of us. Do you agree or disagree? Why?

2. Felix argues that not all successful people need to dress well. In addition to athletes, what professionals might have more freedom when it comes to deciding what to wear?

iQ PRACTICE Go to the online discussion board to discuss the Unit Question with your classmates. *Practice > Unit 2 > Activity 1*

UNIT OBJECTIVE

Listen to a book review and a podcast and gather information and ideas to role-play a conversation offering advice to help someone become better organized.

LISTENING

LISTENING 1 A Perfect Mess

OBJECTIVE ▶ You are going to listen to a review of a book about mess. The book compares people who are neat to people who aren't. It explores who is more successful. As you listen to the review, gather information and ideas about how appearance affects our success.

PREVIEW THE LISTENING

A. PREVIEW Look at the statements below. Check (✓) the statements you agree with.

☐ Messy people are never very organized.

☐ Children should not focus too much on neatness.

☐ Neatness is required in order to work effectively.

☐ It is OK to be a little messy at home.

B. VOCABULARY Read aloud these words from Listening 1. Check (✓) the ones you know. Use a dictionary to define any new or unknown words. Then discuss with a partner how the words will relate to the unit.

bias (n.) OPAL	moderately (adv.)	stifle (v.)
chaos (n.)	open-minded (adj.)	stimulating (adj.)
embrace (v.)	point out (v. phr.)	stumble upon (v. phr.)
inflexible (adj.)	recognize (v.) OPAL	turn out (v. phr.)

🔑 Oxford 5000™ words   **OPAL** Oxford Phrasal Academic Lexicon

28 UNIT 2 How does appearance affect our success?

iQ PRACTICE Go online to listen and practice your pronunciation.
Practice > Unit 2 > Activity 2

WORK WITH THE LISTENING

A. LISTEN AND TAKE NOTES Listen to the review and take notes in the chart.

iQ RESOURCES Go online to download extra vocabulary support.
Resources > Extra Vocabulary > Unit 2

Benefits of being messy	Main ideas and key phrases
At work	
At home	

B. EXPLAIN Imagine you were the police chief in Pennsylvania who was fired because of his messy desk. Use your notes to explain why you should get your job back. Write two or three sentences and share them with a partner.

C. CATEGORIZE Read the statements. Write *T* (true) or *F* (false). Then correct each false statement to make it true.

____ 1. Moderate messiness seems to be good for people.

____ 2. Messy homes are cold and impersonal.

____ 3. Messy environments are not stimulating enough for children.

____ 4. Messy people tend to be more creative and open-minded.

D. IDENTIFY Read the sentences. Then listen again. Circle the answer that best completes each statement.

1. ____ was a very messy but open-minded author.

   a. Albert Einstein

   b. Leon Heppel

   c. Agatha Christie

2. Keeping a house too ____ can be bad for a child's health.

   a. clean

   b. dirty

   c. stimulating

LISTENING 1

3. A messy desk helped ____ two researchers' work.
   a. cause confusion about
   b. show a connection between
   c. find errors in

4. No one interviewed at the NAPO conference could answer the question ____.
   a. "Why are people fined at work?"
   b. "What's wrong with being messy?"
   c. "Why is there a bias toward neatness?"

5. Henry Rubins liked his room to be messy because ____.
   a. chaos made him feel comfortable
   b. he had to be neat at work
   c. it made his mother angry

6. A woman in Australia was fined more than $2,000 because she had ____.
   a. too many personal items on her desk
   b. a lot of papers all over her desk
   c. a messy desk

Leon Heppel

E. CATEGORIZE Read the sentences about the two examples of messy success stories. Who is each sentence about? Write *LH* (Leon Heppel) or *AC* (Agatha Christie).

____ 1. This messy person was a researcher at the National Institutes of Health.

____ 2. This messy person compared the information in two different letters.

____ 3. This messy person wrote ideas in disorganized notebooks.

____ 4. This messy person won a Nobel Prize.

____ 5. This messy person wrote very popular novels.

____ 6. This messy person lost important notebooks in the mess on the desk.

F. VOCABULARY Here are some words from Listening 1. Read the sentences. Circle the answer that best matches the meaning of each bold word or phrase.

1. We hope everyone will **embrace** our new plan for the class trip. We think you will really like the new destination!
   a. be unwilling to accept
   b. accept an idea with enthusiasm
   c. be concerned about

Agatha Christie

VOCABULARY SKILL REVIEW

In Unit 1, you learned about understanding meaning from context. Remember to search the context of an unknown word for clues about its meaning. Look beyond the word's phrase to the sentence or even the text as a whole.

2. I don't want to **stifle** your creativity, but your ideas for the brochure are too complicated. Let's try to make it very simple.
    a. let go of something
    b. prevent something from happening
    c. support something strongly

3. Parents often have a **bias** toward their own children and think they are better than other children.
    a. hope for
    b. a thought about
    c. preference for

4. You need to **point out** in your job application why you think you are qualified for the job. It's important that the interviewer understand your skills and experience.
    a. look at something carefully
    b. make something clear
    c. consider someone's ideas

5. The student was **moderately** successful last semester. He didn't fail any classes, but he didn't get excellent grades, either.
    a. not at all
    b. fairly, but not very
    c. extremely

6. I couldn't find my book, and then I happened to **stumble upon** it at my friend's house. It was there the whole time!
    a. find by accident
    b. hit quickly
    c. damage

7. We worked hard all week, but finally we had to **recognize** that we weren't going to finish the project on time.
    a. acknowledge
    b. discourage
    c. ignore

8. The museum was **stimulating**. I was so excited about what I saw that I went back the next day.
    a. expensive
    b. boring
    c. interesting

9. I was worried, but I think the event will **turn out** fine. It looks like we have everything under control.

   a. increase to a new level

   b. change direction quickly

   c. happen with a particular result

10. I am an **open-minded** person. Just because something is different doesn't mean I won't like it.

    a. afraid of trying new things

    b. careless with someone's property

    c. willing to accept new ideas or opinions

11. The chef is very **inflexible**. He always uses the same recipes. He does not like to try new ideas.

    a. unfriendly to others

    b. unsure of the answer

    c. unwilling to change

12. The little boy's room was complete **chaos**. Books, clothes, and games were scattered all over the floor.

    a. a big mess

    b. orderly and neat

    c. well organized

iQ PRACTICE Go online for more practice with the vocabulary.
Practice › Unit 2 › Activity 3

iQ PRACTICE Go online for additional listening and comprehension.
Practice › Unit 2 › Activity 4

SAY WHAT YOU THINK

DISCUSS Work in a group to discuss the questions.

1. How messy are you? Do you agree with the authors of *A Perfect Mess* about the benefits of being a bit messy? Why or why not?
2. How much freedom to be messy should workers have in their workspace?
3. When you were a child, were you neat or messy? Have you changed at all as you have gotten older? How?

LISTENING SKILL Identifying details

When you listen to a long presentation or lecture, it's difficult to take notes on everything. It's important to focus on details that support the main ideas you hear.

Ask yourself three questions as you listen.

- Is this new information?
- Does this information support the main idea?
- Is this information repeated or rephrased?

If you answer *yes* to any of these questions, the detail may be important to remember.

 A. CATEGORIZE Listen to a short lecture about three strategies for being more organized. Complete the chart with important details about each strategy.

TIP FOR SUCCESS

Use abbreviations and symbols when you take notes. This will make it easier to take notes quickly. Then review your notes to make sure your ideas are clear.

Strategy	Main ideas and key phrases

B. EVALUATE Work with a partner. Compare your notes. Ask each other the following questions. If you answer *no* to a question, revise your notes.

1. Does this information support the main idea?
2. Is this information repeated or rephrased?

iQ PRACTICE Go online for more practice identifying details.
Practice > Unit 2 > Activity 5

NOTE-TAKING SKILL Taking notes to compare and contrast

A T-chart is useful for taking notes about two contrasting topics. When you are reading a text or listening to something about two sides of an issue or two different ideas, make a T-chart by drawing a "T." Write the two topics at the top and make notes under each topic. In some cases, you can write an idea about a topic directly across from the related idea on the other side. Look at the example T-chart below listing some arguments for and against being messy.

Arguments for being messy	Arguments against being messy
• Things can be easier to find because they're right out in the open.	• It's easier to lose or misplace the things we need.
• Being messy can help people connect ideas in new ways.	• Being messy can set a bad example for children.

CATEGORIZE Read and listen to the presentation about the benefits of a happy appearance. Complete the notes in the T-chart on the next page.

ACADEMIC LANGUAGE

It's helpful to listen for key phrases that communicate a contrast. Phrases like *on the other hand*, *at the same time*, *rather than*, and *but in fact* tell the listener that contrasting information is coming up.

_____ OPAL
Oxford Phrasal Academic Lexicon

Sure, we all look better when we smile, but can our facial expressions really cause us to succeed or fail? Many scientists believe that smiling can lead to more success in life, while frowning can lead to more problems. Some researchers discovered that people who smiled in school pictures were more likely to have longer, happier marriages in the future than those who did not. In contrast, people who didn't smile in their class photos tended to get divorced more often. Also, people who smiled in job interviews were more likely to get the jobs than candidates who didn't smile. Smiling also reduces stress, some scientists say. In fact, in one study, smiling while doing a stressful job helped workers' brains and bodies recover from the stress more quickly afterward. On the other hand, people who didn't smile had faster heartbeats long after they finished the stressful job. Maybe this is why smiling can even cause people to live longer. One research study discovered that if baseball players were smiling on their cards, they lived almost seven years longer than players who weren't smiling. So remember to smile!

Happy facial expressions	Serious facial expressions
• longer, happier marriages • more likely to get job after an interview • _____ • _____	• _____ • _____ • more stress • faster heartbeats after stressful job was finished

iQ PRACTICE Go online for more practice taking notes using a T-chart.
Practice > Unit 2 > Activity 6

LISTENING 2   Color Schemes: How Colors Make You Buy

OBJECTIVE ▶ You are going to listen to a podcast from the Canadian Broadcasting Company about how a color can be connected with a particular product, both for consumers and in the law. As you listen to the podcast, gather information and ideas about how a color can lead to the success of a product.

PREVIEW THE LISTENING

A. PREVIEW Before you listen, discuss the questions in a small group.

1. Look at the products and logos. Which ones do you recognize? How important is the color of each one? Does it make the product or logo more recognizable?

2. Colors can communicate different meanings. What do these colors communicate to you? Is your response the same as or different from what the color means to North Americans?

RED (EXCITEMENT, BOLDNESS)
ORANGE (FRIENDSHIP, CONFIDENCE)
YELLOW (OPTIMISM, WARMTH)
GREEN (HEALTH, GROWTH)
BLUE (TRUST, STRENGTH)
PURPLE (CREATIVITY, IMAGINATION)

B. VOCABULARY Read aloud these words from Listening 2. Check (✓) the ones you know. Use a dictionary to define any new or unknown words. Then discuss with a partner how the words will relate to the unit.

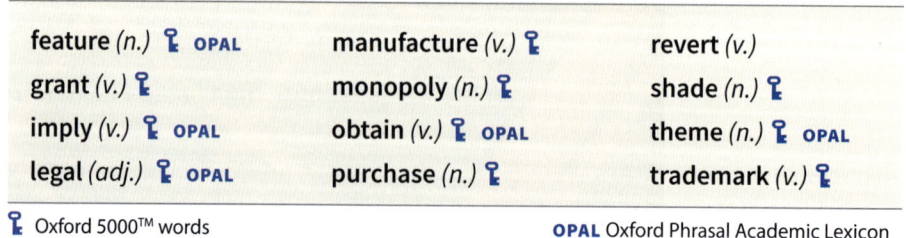

feature (n.) OPAL
grant (v.)
imply (v.) OPAL
legal (adj.) OPAL
manufacture (v.)
monopoly (n.)
obtain (v.) OPAL
purchase (n.)
revert (v.)
shade (n.)
theme (n.) OPAL
trademark (v.)

Oxford 5000™ words   OPAL Oxford Phrasal Academic Lexicon

iQ PRACTICE Go online to listen and practice your pronunciation.
Practice > Unit 2 > Activity 7

36 UNIT 2 How does appearance affect our success?

WORK WITH THE LISTENING

A. LISTEN AND TAKE NOTES Listen to the podcast and take notes on the main ideas in the T-chart.

iQ RESOURCES Go online to download extra vocabulary support.
Resources > Extra Vocabulary > Unit 2

Arguments for color branding	Arguments against color branding

B. EXTEND What are other arguments for and against color branding? Write your ideas in the chart above.

C. EXPLAIN Read the questions. Then listen again. Answer the questions. Compare your answers with a partner.

1. How did Owens Corning's insulation become pink?
2. Why did the courts agree that Owens Corning could protect their pink insulation?
3. How are Tiffany's blue boxes and Louboutin's red shoe soles similar?
4. Where did Louboutin get the idea for his red shoe soles?
5. Why did Louboutin sue Yves Saint Laurent?

D. IDENTIFY Listen to sentences from the podcast. Finish the sentences with the details you hear.

1. Owens Corning made the decision to dye their product red in _____.

2. Then in _____, Owens Corning made legal history when it became the first company to trademark a single color.

3. According to reports, pink insulation commands over _____ percent of the home insulation market.

4. Christian Louboutin is famous for his glamorous shoe designs that cost anywhere from $_____ to _____.

5. The judge also implied that Louboutin's _____ trademark should be canceled.

E. INTERPRET Read the comments below. Match them with the speaker. Would they have been made by workers at Owens Corning (*OC*), Tiffany (*T*), or Louboutin (*L*)? Match them to the workers who would have said them.

____ 1. "Everyone recognizes our boxes and bags immediately because of the distinct color."

____ 2. "We spent money on marketing and even got the Pink Panther to be our mascot."

____ 3. "Our product isn't very exciting, but our consumers ask for us by our color."

____ 4. "Other companies shouldn't be able to use our color. People connect our shade of red directly to our product."

____ 5. "We disagree with the judge's ruling in the Louboutin court case. If they can't trademark red, then our shade of blue is also in danger!"

____ 6. "We use the same color on the soles of all our products because that is how customers can identify our brand."

38 UNIT 2 How does appearance affect our success?

F. EXTEND Work with a partner. Imagine you are judges in the court case between Louboutin and Yves Saint Laurent. Complete the T-chart using points from the listening and your own ideas.

Arguments for allowing Louboutin to trademark shoes with red soles	Arguments for allowing Yves Saint Laurent and other companies to sell shoes with red soles

G. DISCUSS Work in a group. Discuss the questions.

1. The podcast asks if a company should be able to "own" a color? What is your opinion? Explain your reasons.

2. What colors do you connect with products? Why do you think the companies might have chosen those particular colors? Would you change any of the color branding?

H. VOCABULARY Here are some words from Listening 2. Complete each sentence with the correct word.

feature (n.)	legal (adj.)	obtain (v.)	shade (n.)
grant (v.)	manufacture (v.)	purchase (n.)	theme (n.)
imply (v.)	monopoly (n.)	revert (v.)	trademark (v.)

1. They _____ cars at the factory down the street.

2. When I don't know a word in English, I often _____ back to my native language.

3. There are laws to keep any one company from getting a _____ of one area of business.

LISTENING 2 **39**

4. I sent in an application to the bank so I can _____ a credit card.

5. After I made my _____, the cashier wrapped it and put it in a bag.

6. The _____ of the party was the 1970s, so everyone was wearing old clothes.

7. The company wants to _____ the product name so no one else can use it.

8. I want the bank to _____ me a $5,000 loan.

9. I don't want to tell him when he is wrong, but I choose my words carefully so I can _____ it.

10. They got _____ advice from their lawyer.

11. The trees are a beautiful _____ of green.

12. An interesting _____ of our city is the waterfront promenade.

a waterfront promenade

iQ PRACTICE Go online for more practice with the vocabulary.
Practice › Unit 2 › Activity 8

WORK WITH THE VIDEO

A. PREVIEW Can you think of any advantages to being messy? Tell a partner.

VIDEO VOCABULARY

tidy (*adj.*) arranged in good order; neat

effciency (*n.*) the ability to work well without wasting time or energy

clutter (*n.*) things that make a place messy

filthy (*adj.*) dirty

iQ RESOURCES Go online to watch the video about the benefits of being messy. *Resources > Video > Unit 2 > Unit Video*

B. IDENTIFY Watch the video two or three times. Check (✓) the benefits according to the video.

____ Messy people are more relaxed and live longer.

____ Being messy saves time.

____ Messy people get more done.

____ Messy people are more reliable than tidy people.

____ People can find things more easily in a messy office.

____ No one likes to be labeled as organized.

____ Messy people tend to be more expressive.

____ Being messy will help you earn more money at your job.

C. CREATE What could a messy person say in response to the following statement? Use the ideas from the video to write a short response that defends being messy.

"Your desk is really messy. How do you get anything done? I couldn't work like this. I like everything to be in its proper place."

SAY WHAT YOU THINK

SYNTHESIZE Think about Listening 1, Listening 2, and the unit video as you discuss the questions.

1. The speakers suggest that the appearance of a product or a space can send a message. What message do you send by your own appearance and the appearance of your possessions?

2. Think about a time that you judged someone based on how he or she looked or organized things. Was your first impression right or wrong? Why?

3. How can colors help a person to be more organized? How could a productive messy person use color to find things more easily?

VOCABULARY SKILL Using the dictionary: words with multiple definitions

When you look a word up in the dictionary, there are often several different **definitions** given. You must consider the context of the word to choose the correct definition.

Decide what part of speech the word is in that context—for example, a *noun* or a *verb*. When you look up the word, you can then quickly eliminate a form or use of the word not appropriate to the context.

> In many places, casual Fridays are starting to **fade**, and there's a move toward "dress-up" or "formal" Thursdays or Mondays.

fade /feɪd/ *verb* **1** [I, T] to become, or to make something become, paler or less bright: *The curtains had faded in the sun.* ♦ **~ from sth** *All color had faded from her face.* ♦ **~ sth** *The sun had faded the curtains.* ♦ *He was wearing faded blue jeans.* **2** [I] to disappear gradually: *Her smile faded.* ♦ **~ away** *Hopes of reaching an agreement seem to be fading away.* ♦ *The laughter faded away.* ♦ **~ to/into sth** *His voice faded to a whisper* (= gradually became quieter). ♦ *All other issues* **fade into insignificance** *compared with the struggle for survival.* **3** [I] if a sports player, team, actor, etc. **fades**, they stop playing or performing as well as they did before: *Black faded on the final bend.* **IDM** see WOODWORK

Read all of the definitions before you make the choice. By thinking about the context of the report, you can conclude that the first definition of *fade* is not correct in this context.

All dictionary entries adapted from the *Oxford Advanced American Dictionary for learners of English* © Oxford University Press 2011.

A. IDENTIFY Read each sentence. Then circle the correct definition of each bold word.

1. Employees were allowed to **ditch** their suits and ties and formal shirts.

   > **ditch** /dɪtʃ/ noun, verb
   > • **noun** a long channel dug at the side of a field or road, to hold or take away water
   > • **verb 1** [T] ~ **sth/sb** (*informal*) to get rid of something or someone because you no longer want or need it/them: *The new road building program has been ditched.* **2** [T, I] ~ **(sth)** if a pilot **ditches** an aircraft, or if it **ditches**, it lands in the ocean in an emergency **3** [T] ~ **school** (*informal*) to stay away from school without permission

2. A very neat home can be impersonal and **cold**. A messy house can show your personality.

   > **cold** ⚡+ /koʊld/ adj., noun, adv.
   > • **adj.** (**cold·er**, **cold·est**)
   > **> LOW TEMPERATURE 1** having a lower than usual temperature; having a temperature lower than the human body: *I'm cold. Turn the heat up.* ◆ *to feel/look cold* ◆ *cold hands and feet* ◆ *a cold room/house* ◆ *Isn't it cold today?* ◆ *It's freezing cold.* ◆ *to get/turn colder* ◆ *bitterly cold weather* ◆ *the coldest May on record*
   > **> FOOD/DRINKS 2** not heated; cooled after being cooked: *a cold drink* ◆ *Hot and cold food is available in the cafeteria.* ◆ *cold chicken for lunch*
   > **> UNFRIENDLY 3** (of a person) without emotion; unfriendly: *to give someone a cold look/stare/welcome* ◆ *Her manner was cold and distant.* ◆ *He was staring at her with cold eyes.*

B. APPLY Read each sentence. Then look up the definition of the bold word. Write the correct definition for the context of each bold word.

1. I found out how **deep** the world's bias toward neatness and order is.

   _____

2. The woman received a **fine** of more than two thousand dollars at work.

   _____

3. They're looking for a **sign** that people are professional.

   _____

4. I've been messy since I was old enough to **dress** myself.

   _____

iQ PRACTICE Go online for more practice with using the dictionary to check words with multiple definitions. *Practice > Unit 2 > Activity 9*

SPEAKING

OBJECTIVE ▶ At the end of this unit, you are going to role-play a conversation offering advice to help someone become better organized. You will need to be able to confirm understanding during the conversation.

GRAMMAR Subjunctive for suggestions

The **subjunctive** is the simple or base form of a verb—for example, *go* or *try*.

You can use the subjunctive to make a strong suggestion about something that you think should happen.

A sentence with the subjunctive has two clauses: a main clause and a *that* clause.

In the main clause we use a **suggesting verb** or **suggesting expression**.

In the *that* clause we use the **base form of a verb**.

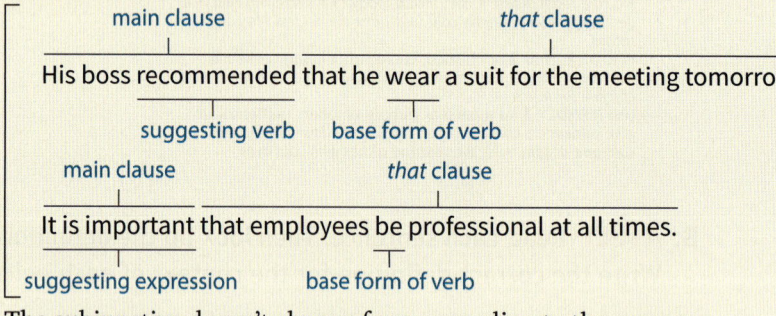

The subjunctive doesn't change form according to the person.

- I recommend that **you work** harder.
- I recommend that **he work** harder.

It also doesn't change tense when the main verb is in the past tense.

- I recommend**ed** that he **work** harder.

To make a negative suggestion, use *not* + the base form of the verb.

- It's essential that employees **not** show up late for meetings.

Certain verbs and certain expressions are often used with the subjunctive to make suggestions and recommendations. The word *that* is optional.

Some verbs followed by the subjunctive	Some expressions followed by the subjunctive
to advise (that)	It's best (that)
to ask (that)	It's desirable (that)
to desire (that)	It's essential (that)
to insist (that)	It's important (that)
to recommend (that)	It's recommended (that)
to request (that)	It's a good idea (that)
to suggest (that)	It's preferred (that)

44 UNIT 2 How does appearance affect our success?

iQ RESOURCES Go online to watch the Grammar Skill Video.
Resources > Video > Unit 2 > Grammar Skill Video

A. RESTATE Rewrite the sentences. Use the subjunctive.

1. Customers expect sales reps to dress more formally.

   Customers request that sales reps _____.

2. Employees should try to avoid looking sloppy at work.

   It is recommended that employees _____.

3. When CEOs pose for a work-related photo, they should not wear jeans and sandals.

   When CEOs pose for a work-related photo, it's important that they

   _____.

4. Some executives want their employees to keep their desks clear of personal items.

   Some executives advise that employees _____

   _____.

5. Some experts say that managers should remind their employees to smile more frequently.

   Some experts suggest that managers _____

   _____.

6. I think that people dressing more formally at work is a good idea.

   It's a good idea that people _____.

B. EXTEND Look at the photos. Write advice for each person on how to dress. Use the subjunctive. Then share your advice with a partner.

A

B

Photo A: This man just started working in a very formal office.

_____

_____

Photo B: This man is going to start working in a casual office.

_____

_____

iQ PRACTICE Go online for more practice with the subjunctive.
Practice > Unit 2 > Activity 10

iQ PRACTICE Go online for the Grammar Expansion: noun clauses.
Practice > Unit 2 > Activity 11

PRONUNCIATION Unstressed syllables

Vowels in stressed syllables are long and clear. In contrast, vowels in unstressed syllables are often reduced to a short sound called a *schwa* (/ə/). It is the most common vowel sound.

Listen to this word.

 appearances

The stressed syllable is the second syllable: *ap-PEAR-an-ces*. The vowel sounds in the unstressed syllables are pronounced /ə/.

/ə·pɪr·ən·səz/

To make the /ə/ sound, drop your jaw a little and relax your tongue. It is a very short, "lazy" sound.

46 UNIT 2 How does appearance affect our success?

TIP FOR SUCCESS

Some online dictionaries have word pronunciations that you can click on. This is a good way to quickly learn the unstressed syllables in new words.

 A. IDENTIFY Listen to the words. Which syllables are unstressed? Cross out the unstressed syllables in each word.

1. pleasure
2. forgotten
3. successful
4. habit
5. business
6. allow
7. cautious
8. professional

 B. APPLY Listen again. Repeat the words. Focus on the unstressed syllables.

iQ PRACTICE Go online for more practice with unstressed syllables. *Practice > Unit 2 > Activity 12*

 CRITICAL THINKING STRATEGY

Restating information

When you **restate** information, you say something again using different words. Restating helps you to understand information, and it shows you what parts you don't understand. Also, restating information helps you to remember it better, so it's a useful study skill.

Restating is different than summarizing. When you restate, you include the same details as the original, but say them in your own words.

iQ PRACTICE Go online to watch the Critical Thinking Video and check your comprehension. *Practice > Unit 2 > Activity 13*

C. RESTATE Read the blog. Tell your partner about one of the points by restating the key information.

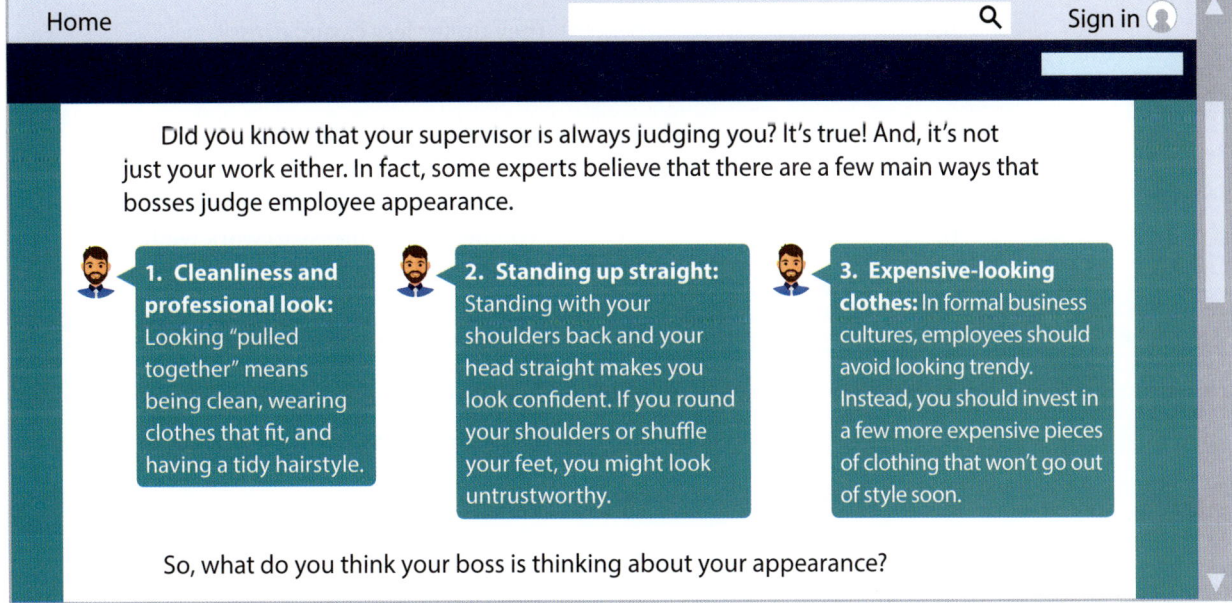

SPEAKING SKILL Confirming understanding

Sometimes you might think that you understand what someone is saying, but you are not exactly sure. These are ways you can check your understanding.

Ask a question that signals your need to confirm your understanding.

Do you mean that . . . ?
Excuse me, are you saying . . . ?
Does that mean . . . ?

Restate what the speaker said in your own words.

If I understand you, . . .
(So) you're saying that . . .

After the speaker responds, let the speaker know that you now understand the information. You can do this by using words or phrases like *thanks*, *OK*, *right*, *I see*, or *got it*.

 A. APPLY Listen to the conversations. Complete the conversations using expressions from the Speaking Skill box. Then practice the conversations with a partner.

TIP FOR SUCCESS

Confirming understanding is a great way to participate actively in a conversation. It shows others you are listening and interested.

1. A: Did you hear that the "Made in Britain" logo is changing from blue and red to gray and red?

   B: What? _____ they're not using the colors in the British flag anymore?

   A: Yes. That's what the news said.

   B: Oh.

2. A: More and more customers are looking for a sign of professionalism.

   B: _____ they prefer less casual dress?

   A: Yeah, that's right.

   B: _____.

3. A: If my desk is too organized, I can't be creative.

   B: _____, you need to be messy to work well?

   A: Yeah, I need a little mess.

   B: _____.

4. A: Most people can't get organized all at once.

   B: _____ it's better to work on it step by step?

   A: Yes, it does.

   B: _____.

B. EXTEND Work in a group. Discuss the questions. Use questions and phrases from the Speaking Skill box to confirm your understanding.

1. What connection is there between appearance and quality of work? Do you think that when people look sloppy, they are less careful at work?

2. Do people's appearance and the condition of their workspace matter if they can get the job done?

3. Do you think that schools should teach students how to be organized?

iQ PRACTICE Go online for more practice confirming understanding. *Practice > Unit 2 > Activity 14*

UNIT ASSIGNMENT Role-play a conversation
OBJECTIVE ▶

In this assignment, you are going to role-play a conversation offering advice to help someone become better organized. As you prepare your role-play, think about the Unit Question, "How does appearance affect our success?" Use information from Listening 1, Listening 2, the unit video, and your work in this unit to support your role-play. Refer to the Self-Assessment checklist on page 50.

CONSIDER THE IDEAS

In a group, list situations that can create a mess at school or work (e.g., piles of paper, not enough storage space). Discuss ways to make the situations better.

PREPARE AND SPEAK

A. GATHER IDEAS Imagine you are in a business to help clients get organized. Read about a new client. Take notes on his situation. Create a T-chart with two columns labeled *Problems* and *Details*.

Name: Dan Howard

Occupation: Sales representative

The Situation: A few years ago, I had the best sales record in my department. My customers respected me, and they were loyal to me. In the past couple of years, however, my sales have dropped. I was doing OK until my manager moved me into a smaller office. There is less storage space for my paperwork. Now I can't find anything. I have piles of customers' papers everywhere. I even lost my phone last week. My old customers don't ask for my help anymore. The few new customers I have don't seem to trust me. I can't blame them. I can't find anything they need. My sales are now the worst in my department. I need help!

SPEAKING 49

B. ORGANIZE IDEAS What advice would you offer to help Dan Howard? Write notes about two or three pieces of advice you would give him. Give details and examples to support your advice.

Advice to improve the situation	Details and examples

C. SPEAK Role-play a conversation with a partner. One person gives advice using the subjunctive when appropriate. The other person role-plays Dan Howard and should confirm understanding. Present the role-play to the class. Refer to the Self-Assessment checklist below before you begin.

iQ PRACTICE Go online for your alternate Unit Assignment.
Practice > Unit 2 > Activity 15

CHECK AND REFLECT

A. CHECK Think about the Unit Assignment as you complete the Self-Assessment checklist.

SELF-ASSESSMENT	Yes	No
I was able to speak easily about the topic.	☐	☐
My partner, group, and class understood me.	☐	☐
I used a T-chart to take notes.	☐	☐
I used the subjunctive.	☐	☐
I used vocabulary from the unit.	☐	☐
I confirmed understanding.	☐	☐
I pronounced unstressed syllables correctly.	☐	☐

B. REFLECT Discuss these questions with a partner or group.

1. What is something new you learned in this unit?

2. Look back at the Unit Question—How does appearance affect our success? Is your answer different now than when you started this unit? If yes, how is it different? Why?

iQ PRACTICE Go to the online discussion board to discuss the questions.
Practice > Unit 2 > Activity 16

TRACK YOUR SUCCESS

iQ PRACTICE Go online to check the words and phrases you have learned in this unit. *Practice > Unit 2 > Activity 17*

Check (✓) the skills and strategies you learned. If you need more work on a skill, refer to the page(s) in parentheses.

LISTENING	☐ I can identify details. (p. 33)
NOTE-TAKING	☐ I can take notes using a T-chart. (p. 34)
VOCABULARY	☐ I can use the dictionary to find multiple definitions of a word. (p. 42)
GRAMMAR	☐ I can use the subjunctive for suggestions. (p. 44)
PRONUNCIATION	☐ I can pronounce unstressed syllables correctly. (p. 46)
CRITICAL THINKING	☐ I can restate information. (p. 47)
SPEAKING	☐ I can confirm understanding. (p. 48)
OBJECTIVE ▶	☐ I can gather information and ideas to role-play a conversation offering advice to help someone become better organized.

SPEAKING **51**

Developmental Psychology

3

NOTE-TAKING	taking notes using key words and phrases
LISTENING	making predictions
CRITICAL THINKING	assessing predictions
VOCABULARY	using the dictionary: words with similar meanings
GRAMMAR	phrasal verbs
PRONUNCIATION	sentence stress
SPEAKING	giving a presentation

 **UNIT QUESTION**

What skills make someone an adult?

A. Discuss these questions with your classmates.

1. In your opinion, at what age does a person become an adult? Why?
2. What important events or experiences can make you feel more like an adult?
3. Look at the photo. What is the woman doing? How does this make her an adult?

B. Listen to *The Q Classroom* online. Then answer these questions.

1. What skills do Felix and Sophy give as examples of adult behavior? Do you agree with them?
2. Marcus recalls a specific event as a turning point between childhood and adulthood. What kinds of skills are involved in hosting a family dinner? How are those skills related to being an adult?

iQ PRACTICE Go to the online discussion board to discuss the Unit Question with your classmates. *Practice › Unit 3 › Activity 1*

UNIT OBJECTIVE

Listen to a lecture, watch a video, and listen to a podcast and gather information and ideas to present a personal story.

NOTE-TAKING SKILL Taking notes using key words and phrases

You can't write down every word as you listen to a lecture or presentation. Speakers may talk too quickly or say things that are not essential to their message. When you take notes, quickly decide which words are important and which words aren't. Write the key words and phrases in your notes.

Here are some tips to help you identify key words and phrases:

- They are directly connected to the topic.
- They communicate the main idea and important supporting details.
- They are usually repeated or rephrased.
- They may be specific names, dates, places, or events.

Do not try to write complete sentences in your notes. Key words and phrases are all you need to help you summarize what you heard.

A. IDENTIFY Listen to the presentation about two ceremonies that celebrate becoming an adult. Check (✓) the key words and phrases. Compare your answers with a partner and explain why you have chosen them.

Ceremony 1	Ceremony 2
☐ very interesting	☐ one tradition
☐ Japan	☐ still popular
☐ special	☐ *Quinceañera*
☐ national holiday	☐ Mexico
☐ second Monday in January	☐ girls
☐ *Seijin no Hi*	☐ celebrate
☐ many young men and women	☐ fifteenth birthday
☐ twenty years old	☐ long, formal dresses
☐ traditional clothes	☐ party
☐ ceremony at government office	☐ dance with their fathers
☐ attend parties with friends	☐ different cultures

B. SUMMARIZE Use your own words to summarize one of the ceremonies discussed in Activity A.

iQ PRACTICE Go online for more practice taking notes using key words and phrases. *Practice > Unit 3 > Activity 2*

Seijin no Hi

Quinceañera

LISTENING

LISTENING 1 "Adulting" School

OBJECTIVE ▶ You are going to listen to a lecture and watch a video news report about a school that teaches young people skills normally associated with being an adult. As you listen to the lecture and watch the video, gather information and ideas about what skills make someone an adult.

PREVIEW THE LISTENING

A. PREVIEW You are going to listen to a lecture about a specific group of adults who don't have a set of skills. Before you listen, discuss the questions in a small group.

1. Look at the names of different generations. Match the names with the years people in each generation were probably born.

Generation X	1920s to 1940s
Generation Z	1940s to 1960s
The Silent Generation	1960s to 1980s
Millennials	1980s to early 2000s
The Baby Boomers	early 2000s to now

2. Which generation do you belong to? What do you know about the characteristics and values of your generation?

LISTENING 1   55

B. VOCABULARY Read aloud these words from Listening 1. Check (✓) the ones you know. Use a dictionary to define any new or unknown words. Then discuss with a partner how the words will relate to the unit.

debt *(n.)* 🔑	minor *(adj.)* 🔑 OPAL	set up *(v. phr.)* 🔑
entrepreneur *(n.)* 🔑	nutrition *(n.)* 🔑	spare *(n.)*
insurance *(n.)* 🔑	precisely *(adv.)* 🔑 OPAL	weigh in *(v. phr.)*
interest *(n.)* 🔑 OPAL	retirement *(n.)* 🔑	

🔑 Oxford 5000™ words   OPAL Oxford Phrasal Academic Lexicon

iQ PRACTICE Go online to listen and practice your pronunciation.
Practice > Unit 3 > Activity 3

WORK WITH THE LISTENING

A. LISTEN AND TAKE NOTES Listen to the lecture. Then watch the video.* Complete the chart with the main points of the lecture and video. Write down only the important words. Compare your notes with a partner.

iQ RESOURCES Go online to watch the video.
Resources > Video > Unit 3 > Listening 1

iQ RESOURCES Go online to download extra vocabulary support.
Resources > Extra Vocabulary > Unit 3

Main ideas	Details
"Adulting" skills—examples?	
How previously learned?	
What is "Adulting" School?	
Why does this appeal to Millennials?	

*Audio version available. *Resources > Audio > Unit 3*

B. IDENTIFY Listen and watch again. Check (✓) the "adulting" skills that the lecture and the video say Millennials might need to learn.

____ 1. searching for a job
____ 2. giving a strong handshake
____ 3. time management
____ 4. minor car repairs
____ 5. buying a home
____ 6. repairing clothing
____ 7. folding a sheet
____ 8. how to pay back student debt
____ 9. speaking a second language
____ 10. giving a speech

C. CATEGORIZE Read the comments about the "Adulting" School. Match each quote with the speaker who probably said it. Compare your answers with a partner.

a. Rachel Weinstein: one of the founders of the "Adulting" School

b. A student at the "Adulting" School

c. A teacher at the "Adulting" School

____ 1. "It's really satisfying to share the basic cooking skills I learned from my mother and grandmother when I was young with a new generation."

____ 2. "I saw an advertisement for an insurance company that offered to teach insurance basics to its customers, and it gave me a great idea that I couldn't wait to share with my friend."

____ 3. "I really want to feel confident when I have to make financial decisions, and I just don't right now. My school didn't offer any classes in budgeting or anything like that."

____ 4. "I know I could watch a video online about some of these things, but it's really great to have a teacher. I can ask questions and post questions in a chat room or by email."

____ 5. "It can be really helpful to know how to take care of your car. I have always saved a lot of money by being able to do some simple things on my own. It's not hard to learn, and I love seeing students' confidence increase."

VOCABULARY SKILL REVIEW

In Unit 2, you learned about how different definitions for a word are appropriate in different contexts. Remember to read all of the dictionary definitions carefully when you are looking up a new word. Think about the context of the unit and the topic of the listening to help you identify the correct definition.

ACADEMIC LANGUAGE

Many words in English have multiple meanings. For instance, you are probably familiar with the most common meaning of the word *interest* (a feeling that you have when you want to know more about somebody or something), but other meanings, such as the one in Listening 1, might be new. An important part of expanding your vocabulary is learning about the additional definitions of the words you already know.

OPAL
Oxford Phrasal Academic Lexicon

D. CATEGORIZE Read the statements. Write *T* (true) or *F* (false). Then correct each false statement to make it true.

____ 1. Millennials are often comfortable with digital technologies.

____ 2. Older people understand why Millennials might want to take "adulting" lessons.

____ 3. The entrepreneurs who started the "Adulting" School teach in a very serious manner.

____ 4. Millennials don't always understand everything associated with paying back a loan.

____ 5. Millennials may have been encouraged to think creatively but not practically.

E. VOCABULARY Here are some words from Listening 1. Complete each sentence with the correct word.

debt *(n.)*	interest *(n.)*	precisely *(adv.)*	spare *(n.)*
entrepreneur *(n.)*	minor *(adj.)*	retirement *(n.)*	weigh in *(v. phr.)*
insurance *(n.)*	nutrition *(n.)*	set up *(v. phr.)*	

1. They looked _____ the same to me.

2. I like my parents to _____ on some decisions before I make them. I find their opinions helpful.

3. I lost my key, so I need to use my _____ to unlock the door.

4. I didn't tell them because it was really a _____ problem. It wasn't serious at all.

5. I need to pay off my _____ to the store. I owe $100.

6. The company was started by two young _____.

7. His dream is to _____ his own business.

8. I don't like to borrow money because I hate to pay all the _____.

9. Good _____ is an important part of a healthy lifestyle.

10. The car was damaged in the accident, but we have _____ that will pay for the repairs.

11. At 60, he will soon be approaching _____ age.

58   UNIT 3   What skills make someone an adult?

iQ PRACTICE Go online for more practice with the vocabulary.
Practice > Unit 3 > Activity 4

iQ PRACTICE Go online for additional listening and comprehension.
Practice > Unit 3 > Activity 5

SAY WHAT YOU THINK

DISCUSS Work in a group to discuss the questions.

1. What are the skills from Listening 1 that you associate with adulthood? Can you think of any others that were not mentioned?

2. Can you remember an event or experience that made you feel like you had become an adult? What skills did you need at that time?

LISTENING SKILL Making predictions

Predictions are guesses you make based only on the information that is available. For example, you may know the title of a lecture. You can use the title to predict the topic and the ideas it might cover.

Your predictions are also based on what you already know about a topic. Background information from articles you have read, from electronic media, and from previous experiences all help prepare you to understand new information, and to predict what you are likely to hear next.

One way to make predictions is to write down the topic. Then take brief notes on the ideas and vocabulary you already know that are associated with that topic. This prepares you for the information that you will hear, so you don't have to work quite as hard to understand it.

TIP FOR SUCCESS

Graphic organizers work well for making predictions. Web diagrams are very useful. Write the topic in a circle in the center. Write notes about your predictions and possible vocabulary on lines coming from the center.

A. APPLY Read the lecture titles. Predict the topic of the lecture and the main ideas it might cover. Write brief notes about what you already know about each topic. Then list five words you might expect to hear about it.

1. Trends in World Architecture (*Architecture Appreciation Lecture*)
2. Global Warming (*Environmental Studies*)
3. Technology in Schools (*Media Studies*)

B. IDENTIFY Read the questions. Then listen to the excerpts. Circle the correct answers.

1. Which of the following is most likely to be discussed in the lecture?
   a. what to do when you want a promotion
   b. how to explain your side of an argument
   c. what kinds of jobs are right for you

2. What is Adam most likely to suggest?
   a. Don't take the online class that I took.
   b. You should focus on your job.
   c. Schedule some time every night just for homework.

3. What is Tara most likely to say next?
   a. "You're going to have a wonderful time."
   b. "You still owe me some money."
   c. "You were never very nice to me."

4. How will the employees most likely feel when they hear the news?
   a. worried
   b. confused
   c. excited

iQ PRACTICE Go online for more practice listening to make predictions.
Practice > Unit 3 > Activity 6

UNIT 3 What skills make someone an adult?

CRITICAL THINKING STRATEGY

Assessing predictions

While making predictions is a useful listening skill, it's important not only to make the predictions but also to assess how accurate your predictions are so you can make better predictions moving forward. Here are helpful steps for assessing your predictions:

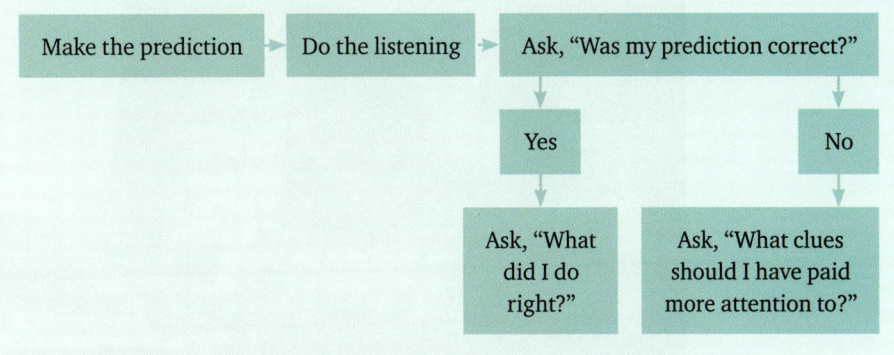

iQ PRACTICE Go online to watch the Critical Thinking Video and check your comprehension. *Practice > Unit 3 > Activity 7*

 C. IDENTIFY Work with a partner. Look at the lecture title. Predict the main ideas it might cover. Then listen to the beginning of the lecture. Circle the ideas that you correctly predicted.

Water Shortages: The Causes of a Global Crisis (Geography Lecture)

What I think the main ideas might be: _____

_____

_____

D. ANALYZE Discuss these questions about your predictions in Activity C.

1. How did you correctly guess the main ideas?

2. Why were some of your guesses incorrect?

E. ANALYZE Look back at your predictions in Activity A on page 59. Look at the main ideas you thought you might hear. Circle the ones that were in the lectures. Then ask yourself what you did right and how you can make better predictions in the future.

LISTENING 2 Financial Literacy Among Young People

OBJECTIVE ▶ You are going to listen to a podcast from the Canadian Broadcasting Company about financial knowledge among young people. As you listen to the podcast, gather information and ideas about what skills make someone an adult.

PREVIEW THE LISTENING

A. PREVIEW Before you listen, read the title of the podcast and look at the photo above. What predictions can you make about what the speaker might say? Discuss your ideas with a partner.

B. VOCABULARY Read aloud these words from Listening 2. Check (✓) the ones you know. Use a dictionary to define any new or unknown words. Then discuss with a partner how the words will relate to the unit.

agency (n.) 🔑	mortgage (n.) 🔑	stock (n.) 🔑 OPAL
asset (n.) 🔑	naturally (adv.) 🔑 OPAL	tool (n.) 🔑 OPAL
balance (v.) 🔑 OPAL	pension (n.) 🔑	tedious (adj.)
current (adj.) 🔑 OPAL	series (n.) 🔑 OPAL	truly (adv.) 🔑

🔑 Oxford 5000™ words   **OPAL** Oxford Phrasal Academic Lexicon

iQ PRACTICE Go online to listen and practice your pronunciation.
Practice > Unit 3 > Activity 8

WORK WITH THE LISTENING

🔊 **A. LISTEN AND TAKE NOTES** Listen to the podcast and read the notes. Cross out the words that are not important. Compare your answers with a partner.

iQ RESOURCES Go online to download extra vocabulary support.
Resources > Extra Vocabulary > Unit 3

A man and woman went to the bank to get a mortgage.

The banker talked about a lot of financial things.

The man fell asleep.

The man was bored because he was financially illiterate.

The man doesn't understand the first thing about finances.

Forbes magazine reported that teenagers are dangerously financially illiterate.

It is killing us.

Young people don't know the difference between an asset and a liability.

This is happening in the US and in Canada.

The government in Canada started the Financial Consumer Agency of Canada in 2001.

Its job is to teach young people about finances.

It has a month—November—to promote financial literacy.

Schools in Ontario have started to talk about money to children in elementary school.

B. APPLY Use your notes to summarize the main ideas of the podcast. Complete the sentences.

1. Many young people _____.

2. The solution to the problem seems to be _____.

C. ANALYZE Think about your predictions from Activity A on page 59. Were any of your predictions correct? If so, how did you make those predictions? What will help you make better predictions in the future?

D. CATEGORIZE Read the statements. Then listen again. Write *T* (true) or *F* (false). Then correct each false statement to make it true.

____ 1. Banks make the speaker feel relaxed.

____ 2. *Forbes* magazine is worried about the state of financial literacy among young people.

____ 3. Students remember financial literacy lessons for about two years.

____ 4. The speaker had a savings account when he was a child where he saved his allowance.

____ 5. The speaker's dream salary was $100,000.

____ 6. The Financial Consumer Agency of Canada's only job is to teach young people about finances.

____ 7. The Financial Consumer Agency of Canada thinks financial literacy is important.

____ 8. The speaker is sure he would be financially literate if he had studied finances when he was young.

E. CATEGORIZE Read about some choices young people made. Do they seem financially literate or financially illiterate? Write *L* for financially literate and *I* for financially illiterate. Compare answers with a partner.

_____ 1. "I got a really big student loan so I could quit my job and relax more between classes. I'll pay it back someday when I get a really good job. I'm not worried at all."

_____ 2. "The bank offered us a really big mortgage, but we wanted to make sure we could afford the monthly payments without changing our lifestyle. We actually borrowed less money than the bank offered."

_____ 3. "I earn a pretty good paycheck, and I like to shop and have fun. I don't usually save money because somehow it's just all gone by the time I get paid again."

_____ 4. "I am too busy to make a financial retirement plan for my future. I am sure things will work out OK. I will have children, and they will take care of me. I don't need to think about it now."

_____ 5. "I try to pay off my credit card debt every month. I really don't like to owe money, and I hate paying interest. It's like throwing money into the garbage can."

_____ 6. "I want to buy a new smartphone, but I don't have enough money right now. I'm going to save some money each month, and in a few months, I'll have enough."

F. DISCUSS Work in groups to discuss the questions.

1. Were you surprised to hear that financial illiteracy is so high among young people? Why or why not?

2. Think about your own financial literacy. What do you know about? Circle the topics you feel confident talking about.

buying a house	investments	repaying a loan
credit cards	making a budget	retirement savings
credit scores	making smart purchases	saving for emergencies
insurance		

G. VOCABULARY Here are some words from Listening 2. Read the sentences. Then write each bold word next to the correct definition.

1. It was a **truly** wonderful evening.
2. He works for the government at the Environmental Protection **Agency**.
3. We took out for a **mortgage** to buy our new house.
4. When he retired from work at 65 years old, he started to receive a **pension**.
5. If you don't **balance** your finances by doing a budget every month, you might be spending more than you are earning.
6. She makes a financial plan for each year, and now she is working on a budget for the **current** year.
7. The computer is a valuable **tool** used by almost every profession.
8. The school is offering a **series** of classes on financial literacy. You can sign up for all of them now or one at a time.
9. A strong runner is an **asset** to a football team.
10. **Naturally**, I get upset when things go wrong.
11. I wish I had bought **stocks** in Apple when they were first offered. I would be really rich now.
12. I find sewing to be very **tedious** work. It's dull and too detailed for me.

a. _____ (v.) to show that in a bank account the total money spent is equal to the total money received

b. _____ (adj.) boring

c. _____ (n.) a thing that helps you to do your job or to achieve something

d. _____ (n.) money paid regularly by a government or company to somebody who is considered to be too old or too ill/sick to work

e. _____ (adj.) of the present time

f. _____ (adv.) in a way that you would expect

g. _____ (adv.) used to emphasize a particular quality

h. _____ (n.) a person or thing that is valuable

i. _____ (n.) a government department that provides a particular service

j. _____ (*n.*) several events or things of a similar kind that happen one after the other

k. _____ (*n.*) a legal agreement by which a bank or similar organization lends you money to buy a house and you pay the money back over a particular number of years

l. _____ (*n.*) a share that somebody has bought in a company or business

iQ PRACTICE Go online for more practice with the vocabulary.
Practice > Unit 3 > Activity 9

SAY WHAT YOU THINK

SYNTHESIZE Think about Listening 1 and Listening 2 as you discuss the questions.

1. Who should be responsible for teaching young people important life skills? Their parents? Schools? The government? Private institutions?

2. Do you think these skills really make someone a successful adult? If yes, why? If no, what skills might be more important?

VOCABULARY SKILL Using the dictionary: words with similar meanings

There are many words that have similar meanings but are not exactly the same. For example, both *adolescence* and *youth* can be used for the time between childhood and adulthood. Read the following definitions.

> **ad·o·les·cence** /ˌædlˈɛsns/ *noun* [U] the time in a person's life when he or she develops from a child into an adult
> **SYN** PUBERTY ⊃ collocations at AGE

> **youth** ⫽+ /yuθ/ *noun* (*pl.* **youths** /yuðz; yuθs/) **1** [U] the time of life when a person is young, especially the time before a child becomes an adult.

The dictionary definitions show that although the words are very similar, *adolescence* describes a more specific time period, while *youth* is more general.

Checking the definitions of similar words can help you determine which word is appropriate in a context.

All dictionary entries adapted from the *Oxford Advanced American Dictionary for learners of English* © Oxford University Press 2011.

A. APPLY Read the dictionary definitions of words from this unit and their synonyms. Complete each sentence with the correct word.

1. a. If you are having trouble managing your money, you should go to the bank to get some _____ advice.

   b. Countries such as India and China have experienced rapid _____ growth in recent years.

> **ec·o·nom·ic** /ˌɛkəˈnɑmɪk; ˌikə-/ adj.
> **1** [only before noun] connected with the trade, industry, and development of wealth of a country, an area, or a society: *social, economic and political issues*

> **fi·nan·cial** /fəˈnænʃl; faɪ-/ adj. [usually before noun]
> connected with money and finance: *financial services* • *to give financial advice* • *to be in financial difficulties*

2. a. The lawyer can _____ that the man is guilty of the crime by recreating the events of the day.

   b. The report _____ us that there is still a lot of work to do.

> **dem·on·strate** /ˈdɛmənˌstreɪt/ verb
> **1** [T] to show something clearly by giving proof or evidence: ~ **that**…*These results demonstrate convincingly that our campaign is working.* • ~ **sth (to sb)** *Let me demonstrate to you some of the difficulties we are facing.*

> **show** /ʃoʊ/ verb, noun
> • verb (showed, shown /ʃoʊn/ or, rarely, showed)
> **> MAKE CLEAR 1** [T] to make something clear; to prove something: ~ **(that)**…*The figures clearly show that her claims are false.* • ~ **sb that**… *Market research has shown us that people want quality, not just low prices.* • ~ **sth**… *a report showing*

B. COMPOSE Look up the definitions of these pairs of words. Write an appropriate sentence using each word. Take turns reading your sentences to a partner.

1. assume / suppose (v.)

2. age / mature (v.)

3. response / reply (n.)

4. order / instruct (v.)

5. cover / hide (v.)

iQ PRACTICE Go online for more practice using the dictionary to check words with similar meanings. *Practice > Unit 3 > Activity 10*

SPEAKING

OBJECTIVE ▶ At the end of this unit, you are going to present a personal story describing an important event in your life that made you feel like an adult. In order to tell your story, you will need to follow the appropriate steps for giving a presentation.

GRAMMAR Phrasal verbs

Phrasal verbs are verbs that consist of two words used together. The first word is a verb and the second word is called a *particle*. Particles sometimes look like prepositions, but they have different meanings. The verb and the particle together make a new meaning. For example, *take on* is a phrasal verb. When you put the words *take* and *on* together, they mean "to accept."

- He **took on** a lot of responsibilities.

There are two kinds of phrasal verbs: *transitive* and *intransitive*.

Transitive Phrasal Verbs

A transitive phrasal verb requires a direct object.

- He **picked up** his brother from school.
  verb   particle   object

Most transitive phrasal verbs are *separable*. This means the direct object can also go between the verb and the particle.

- He **picked** his brother **up** from school.
  verb   object   particle

When the direct object is a pronoun, it must go between the verb and the particle.

- ✓ He **picked** him **up** from school.
- ✗ He **picked up** him from school.

Some transitive phrasal verbs are inseparable. This means the direct object cannot go between the verb and the particle.

- ✓ My mother is busy today, so I'll **look after** the baby.
- ✗ My mother is busy today, so I'll **look** the baby **after**.

Intransitive Phrasal Verbs

Intransitive phrasal verbs don't take a direct object at all. They are never separable.

- In some situations, children **grow up** faster than in others.

It can be difficult to understand the meaning of a phrasal verb by looking at the words that make it up. Also, some phrasal verbs have more than one meaning. When you learn a new phrasal verb's meaning, you must also learn if it is transitive or intransitive and whether it is separable or inseparable.

iQ RESOURCES Go online to watch the Grammar Skill Video.
Resources > Video > Unit 3 > Grammar Skill Video

A. IDENTIFY Listen to the sentences with phrasal verbs. Write the particles you hear.

1. grow _____
2. weigh _____
3. pay _____
4. sneak education _____
5. figure it _____
6. drop _____ on

TIP FOR SUCCESS

In the dictionary, phrasal verbs are usually located with the definition(s) of the verb in the phrasal verb. Many dictionaries also have example sentences that follow the definitions. Example sentences are an easy way to see if a phrasal verb is *transitive* or *intransitive* and *separable* or *inseparable*.

B. CATEGORIZE Read the sentences. Underline each phrasal verb. Write *T* (transitive) or *I* (intransitive).

____ 1. I don't know what to do about this problem, but we need to work it out.

____ 2. I waved goodbye to my parents and got on a plane.

____ 3. Lessons about financial literacy are going on all over Canada these days.

____ 4. Many children all over the world have to give their childhoods up early and go to work.

____ 5. Adults need to know how to take care of living things like pets or plants and ultimately maybe children.

____ 6. Being an adult means getting out of bed when your baby is crying even when you are really tired.

iQ PRACTICE Go online for more practice with phrasal verbs.
Practice > Unit 3 > Activity 11

iQ PRACTICE Go online for the Grammar Expansion: phrasal verbs with different meanings. *Practice > Unit 3 > Activity 12*

PRONUNCIATION Sentence stress

Words in a sentence are not pronounced with equal stress. Words that contain important information, called **content words**, are said with more stress. They are longer, louder, higher pitched, and clearer. Words that serve a grammatical purpose are called **function words**. They are usually unstressed.

Stressing words focuses the listener's attention on the most important ideas in sentences. Using sentence stress correctly makes it easier to communicate your ideas.

Content words: usually stressed		Function words: usually unstressed	
Nouns	father, Tuesday, etc.	Articles	a, an, the
Main verbs	come, walks, etc.	Auxiliary verbs	be, have, can, etc.
Adjectives	beautiful, red, etc.	Prepositions	in, at, etc.
Adverbs	quickly, very, etc.	Personal pronouns	I, you, me, etc.
Negatives	not, can't, etc.	Possessive pronouns	my, your, his, etc.
Question words	where, how, etc.	Relative pronouns	that, which, who, etc.
Demonstrative pronouns	this, that, etc.	Short connector words	and, so, when, then, etc.

For example, listen to the following sentence. The underlined words are stressed.

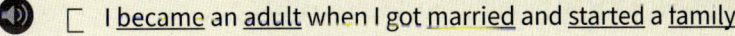
I <u>became</u> an <u>adult</u> when I got <u>married</u> and <u>started</u> a <u>family</u>.

A. ANALYZE Listen to the sentences. Underline the stressed words you hear. Then practice saying the sentences with a partner.

1. When you become employed, you can call yourself an adult.
2. I think it's how much you can provide for yourself.
3. I think it's when you get married.
4. I think you become an adult at 16.
5. The day that I'm an adult is the day that I can do whatever I want to do.
6. The age at which you become an adult varies.

B. CATEGORIZE Underline the important content words in the conversation. Then work with a partner to read the conversation. Stress the content words.

A: Congratulations!

B: Thanks! I can't believe I've graduated already.

A: Yeah. You're an adult now!

B: But I don't feel like an adult. I don't think I learned the right skills in school.

A: Really? Well, I have been taking care of my younger siblings for years now, and I learned a lot of things the hard way.

B: I still rely on my parents a lot.

A: Well, maybe that will change now that you've graduated!

iQ PRACTICE Go online for more practice with sentence stress.
Practice > Unit 3 > Activity 13

SPEAKING SKILL Giving a presentation

When you give a presentation, it is important to look and feel confident. People will be more interested in your ideas if they see that you believe in yourself and your ideas. Here are some steps to follow.

Before you give your presentation

1. Make sure you can clearly pronounce all the key words in your speech. Concentrate on proper word stress.

2. Make sure your notes are well organized. Memorize the main points of your speech so that you won't need to read your presentation. You want to look at your audience, not down at your notes.

3. Practice your presentation several times. Practice in front of a mirror and in front of a friend or family member.

When you begin your presentation

1. Introduce yourself clearly and confidently.

2. Remember to smile.

During your presentation

1. Make eye contact with members of the audience. You want them to feel you want to communicate with each of them.

2. Think about your hand gestures and posture as you speak. You want to appear relaxed and in control. If you move too much, or too little, you will appear nervous. Use gestures for emphasis and to make your points clearer.

A. CREATE Listen to a presentation about becoming an adult. Then list five suggestions you would give the speaker. Compare your suggestions with a partner.

Suggestions:

1. _____
_____

2. _____
_____

3. _____
_____

4. _____
_____

5. _____
_____

B. SYNTHESIZE Create a brief presentation to tell about one important event in your life. Practice the presentation once and then present it to a partner. Take note of the suggestions your partner gives you. Take turns presenting and giving suggestions.

iQ PRACTICE Go online for more practice giving a presentation.
Practice › Unit 3 › Activity 14

UNIT ASSIGNMENT Give a presentation to a group

OBJECTIVE ▶

In this section, you will give a short presentation about a personal story. As you prepare your presentation, think about the Unit Question, "What skills make someone an adult"? Use information from Listening 1, Listening 2, and your work in this unit to support your presentation. Refer to the Self-Assessment checklist on page 76.

CONSIDER THE IDEAS

 A. LISTEN AND TAKE NOTES Listen to one person's story about a skill he had to learn as he became an adult. Take notes as you listen.

1. What important event became a turning point in the speaker's life?	
2. What dream did the speaker give up?	
3. What skill did he learn that made him feel more grown up?	

B. DISCUSS Work with a partner. Compare your notes and discuss the speaker's main points.

PREPARE AND SPEAK

TIP FOR SUCCESS

When you are brainstorming, no idea is a bad idea. Write down any ideas you have.

A. GATHER IDEAS Brainstorm about important skills you gained that made you feel more like an adult. Make notes in the spider map.

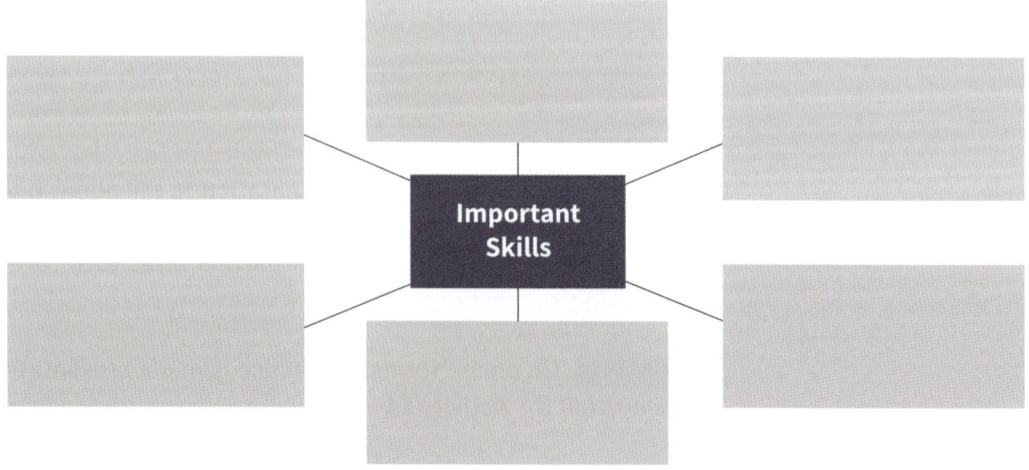

74 UNIT 3 What skills make someone an adult?

B. ORGANIZE IDEAS Complete these activities.

1. Choose one event to use for your presentation.

2. Use the chart to organize your ideas. It is not necessary to write full sentences. Just write notes. Try to include some phrasal verbs in your presentation.

Introduction (main idea)

Important ideas and details

Conclusion

3. Work with a partner to practice your presentation until you can answer *yes* to the following questions.

   a. Did you introduce yourself clearly?

   b. Did you pronounce all the key words correctly?

   c. Did you use stress correctly?

   d. Did you use your notes to tell your ideas rather than read them?

   e. Did you make eye contact?

   f. Did you use relaxed gestures?

   g. Did you smile?

C. SPEAK Present your personal story. Follow these steps. Refer to the Self-Assessment checklist below before you begin.

1. Work in a group. Take turns presenting your personal stories.

2. Pay attention to how your classmates make their presentations. Try to make predictions about what they will say. Offer suggestions to group members when they complete their presentations.

iQ PRACTICE Go online for your alternate Unit Assignment.
Practice > Unit 3 > Activity 15

CHECK AND REFLECT

A. CHECK Think about the Unit Assignment as you complete the Self-Assessment checklist.

SELF-ASSESSMENT	Yes	No
I was able to speak easily about the topic.	☐	☐
I took notes using key words and phrases.	☐	☐
My partner, group, and class understood me.	☐	☐
I made predictions about the presentations.	☐	☐
I used vocabulary from the unit.	☐	☐
I gave a presentation.	☐	☐
I used sentence stress correctly.	☐	☐

B. REFLECT Discuss these questions with a partner or group.

1. What is something new you learned in this unit?

2. Look back at the Unit Question—What skills make someone an adult? Is your answer different now than when you started this unit? If yes, how is it different? Why?

iQ PRACTICE Go to the online discussion board to discuss the questions.
Practice > Unit 3 > Activity 16

TRACK YOUR SUCCESS

iQ PRACTICE Go online to check the words and phrases you have learned in this unit. *Practice > Unit 3 > Activity 17*

Check (✓) the skills and strategies you learned. If you need more work on a skill, refer to the page(s) in parentheses.

NOTE-TAKING	☐ I can take notes using key words and phrases. (p. 54)
LISTENING	☐ I can make predictions. (p. 59)
CRITICAL THINKING	☐ I can assess my predictions for accuracy. (p. 61)
VOCABULARY	☐ I can use the dictionary to check the definitions of words with similar meanings to fit a context. (p. 67)
GRAMMAR	☐ I can use phrasal verbs. (p. 69)
PRONUNCIATION	☐ I can use appropriate sentence stress. (p. 71)
SPEAKING	☐ I can give a presentation. (p. 72)
OBJECTIVE ▶	☐ I can gather information and ideas to present a personal story describing an important event in my life.

Science

NOTE-TAKING	using a split page
LISTENING	making inferences
VOCABULARY	word forms
CRITICAL THINKING	distinguishing between similar words
GRAMMAR	present perfect and present perfect continuous
PRONUNCIATION	basic intonation patterns
SPEAKING	avoiding answering questions

 **UNIT QUESTION**

How do the laws of science affect our lives?

A. Discuss these questions with your classmates.

1. Which science subject did you like best in school: biology, chemistry, or physics? Why?
2. The laws of science describe natural events. What laws of science do you know about?
3. Look at the photo. When a rocket is launched, it demonstrates Newton's third law of motion. What do you think that law says?

B. Listen to *The Q Classroom* online. Then match the laws in the box with the students who talked about them.

a. Archimedes's buoyancy principle
b. Newton's law of gravitation
c. Newton's third law of motion

Marcus	
Sophy	
Yuna	
Felix	

iQ PRACTICE Go to the online discussion board to discuss the Unit Question with your classmates. *Practice > Unit 4 > Activity 1*

UNIT OBJECTIVE ▶ Listen to a class discussion, watch a video, and listen to a lecture. Gather information and ideas to create a role-play about presenting a business plan for a new product.

NOTE-TAKING SKILL Using a split page

Using a split-page method to take notes can help you better understand and remember information. To use the split-page method, divide your page into two sections by folding it lengthwise. Write your notes about main ideas and important details in the section on the right. After you have listened, read your notes and write questions about what you heard in the section on the left. You can write questions that are answered in your notes, questions you think might be asked on a quiz or test, or questions you would like to find answers to.

Questions	Notes on main ideas and important details

A. APPLY Listen to a podcast about a new invention, BEACON, that uses the ocean as a power source. Use the right side of the page to take notes about the main ideas and important details you hear.

Hannah Herbst and BEACON

Questions	Notes on main ideas and important details
	_____—Hannah Herbst
	_____—Bringing Electricity Access to Countries through Ocean Energy
	Appearance: _____ _____ _____
	What it does: _____ _____
	Hydropower—Newton's _____
	When _____ hit the _____, they move.
	When the _____ move, they make a generator turn, which makes _____.

B. COMPOSE Review your notes from Activity A. Write questions about the notes in the section on the left.

iQ PRACTICE Go online for more practice using a split page to take notes and create questions. *Practice > Unit 4 > Activity 2*

80   UNIT 4   How do the laws of science affect our lives?

LISTENING

LISTENING 1 Gravity at Work

OBJECTIVE ▶ You are going to listen to a discussion in a physics class. As you listen, gather information and ideas about how the laws of science affect our lives.

PREVIEW THE LISTENING

A. PREVIEW Look at the picture above. Have you seen this item before? What might it be used for? Why do you think it was invented? Share your ideas with a partner.

B. VOCABULARY Read aloud these words from Listening 1. Check (✓) the ones you know. Use a dictionary to define any new or unknown words. Then discuss with a partner how the words will relate to the unit.

affordable *(adj.)* 🗝	intention *(n.)* 🗝 OPAL
alternative *(n.)* 🗝 OPAL	inventor *(n.)*
force *(n.)* 🗝 OPAL	power *(v.)* 🗝
function *(v.)* 🗝 OPAL	stream *(v.)*
gear *(n.)* 🗝	summarize *(v.)* 🗝 OPAL
hazardous *(adj.)*	throughout *(prep.)* 🗝 OPAL

🗝 Oxford 5000™ words   **OPAL** Oxford Phrasal Academic Lexicon

iQ PRACTICE Go online to listen and practice your pronunciation.
Practice ▶ Unit 4 ▶ Activity 3

WORK WITH THE LISTENING

A. LISTEN AND TAKE NOTES Listen to the discussion. Complete the notes in the right column of the chart.

iQ RESOURCES Go online to download extra vocabulary support.
Resources > Extra Vocabulary > Unit 4

Questions	Notes
	GravityLight
	_____ Reeves and Riddiford
	wanted to find _____
	works by _____
	gear inside GL _____
	Mr. Trash Wheel
	Baltimore has had a problem with _____
	invented by Kellett— _____
	description: _____
	how it works: _____

B. COMPOSE Read your notes and in the left column write questions about what you heard.

C. IDENTIFY Read the questions. Then listen again. Circle the correct answers.

1. Why does a pencil move toward the ground when you drop it?
   a. Because gravity attracts the smaller object to the bigger object
   b. Because a pencil is heavier than the air around it
2. Where are kerosene lights commonly used?
   a. In England
   b. In the developing world
3. Why did Reeves and Riddiford want to invent a light without a battery?
   a. Batteries contain dangerous chemicals.
   b. Batteries are expensive.
4. How many minutes of light does the GravityLight provide?
   a. 12 minutes
   b. 20 minutes
5. What caused Kellett to invent Mr. Trash Wheel?
   a. He was tired of his workplace being disgusting.
   b. He wanted a partnership with Baltimore City.
6. How much garbage has Mr. Trash Wheel kept out of the harbor?
   a. About a million pounds
   b. More than a million pounds

kerosene lamp

D. CATEGORIZE Read the statements. Write *T* (true) or *F* (false). Then correct each false statement to make it true.

____ 1. Kerosene lights are dirty, dangerous, and expensive.
____ 2. GravityLight is a light attached to a weight that slowly falls and powers the light.
____ 3. The parts for GravityLight are cheap, so it isn't an expensive product.
____ 4. Reeves and Riddiford think their light can help people throughout the world.
____ 5. Baltimore's trash comes from people throwing it in the street and from the wind blowing it out of garbage cans.
____ 6. Mr. Trash Wheel relies only on gravity to function.
____ 7. Mr. Trash Wheel collects trash in good and bad weather.

E. EXTEND Discuss the questions in a group.

1. What are some problems Reeves and Riddiford might face when they try to sell GravityLight?
2. Why do you think Kellett added the eyes to the top of Mr. Trash Wheel?
3. Would it surprise you to learn that Mr. Trash Wheel has become a tourist attraction in Baltimore? Why do you think that might be?

F. VOCABULARY Here are some words from Listening 1. Complete each sentence with the correct word.

affordable *(adj.)*	function *(v.)*	intention *(n.)*	stream *(v.)*
alternative *(n.)*	gear *(n.)*	inventor *(n.)*	summarize *(v.)*
force *(n.)*	hazardous *(adj.)*	power *(v.)*	throughout *(prep.)*

1. When you cry, tears _____ down your face.
2. The electric company makes enough energy to _____ the town.
3. Don't tell me the whole story. Just _____ it.
4. That jacket is too expensive. I need to find one that is more _____.
5. I can't ride my bicycle because the _____ is broken.
6. The _____ of the moving water pushes the wheel around.
7. I like to think about every _____ before I make a decision.
8. It's illegal to dump _____ chemicals in rivers and lakes.
9. Alexander Graham Bell was an important _____. When he made the first telephone, he changed history forever.
10. When designed well, a video game can _____ as an educational tool.
11. She is working with the _____ of saving money to pay for college.
12. There was art _____ the entire museum. Paintings, photographs, and sculptures were in every room.

waterwheel

84 UNIT 4 How do the laws of science affect our lives?

iQ PRACTICE Go online for more practice with the vocabulary.
Practice > Unit 4 > Activity 4

iQ PRACTICE Go online for additional listening and comprehension.
Practice > Unit 4 > Activity 5

SAY WHAT YOU THINK

DISCUSS Work in a group to discuss the questions.

1. If you could choose which product to invest in, would you choose GravityLight or Mr. Trash Wheel? Why?

2. What other products do you know about like GravityLight that inventors have created from simple parts to help people in developing areas?

3. Would Mr. Trash Wheel be welcome in your city? Why or why not?

LISTENING SKILL Making inferences

We often understand ideas that the speaker has not actually stated. **Making inferences** involves "reading between the lines," or figuring out more than is actually said to understand the full meaning. Listen carefully to make inferences based on the information available to you.

In the excerpt below, the speaker, Rowan, tells us about the invention of Mr. Trash Wheel.

> So, this guy, John Kellett, is a sailor and an engineer in Baltimore. He worked for years in the harbor. He was tired of seeing all the garbage in the water, so he worked with the Waterfront Partnership of Baltimore to build a trash wheel.

Based on this information, we can infer that Mr. Trash Wheel was John Kellett's idea and that the Waterfront Partnership of Baltimore helped him to build it.

Often, speakers communicate how they feel about the ideas they are presenting. To fully understand someone, listen closely to infer attitudes and emotions. Pay attention to the following.

Speed and pitch: If a speaker is talking quickly, and his or her pitch goes up and down, this may indicate that the speaker is excited or passionate about the topic.

Tone: Does the speaker laugh or sound serious?

Descriptive words: Listen for words that express feelings and opinions, like *love, hate, terrible, wonderful, terrific,* and so on.

A. EVALUATE Listen to excerpts from Listening 1. Based on the statements in each excerpt, what can you infer? Circle the correct answers.

Excerpt 1

a. The professor believes the students understand.

b. The professor isn't sure if the students understand.

Excerpt 2

a. The students were free to organize their presentations in the way that made sense to them.

b. The students should have organized their presentations in a particular way.

Excerpt 3

a. Kerosene lights are cheap.

b. Kerosene lights are efficient.

B. IDENTIFY Listen to the excerpts from Listening 1. Circle the correct answers.

1. In Excerpt 1, you can infer that the speaker is ____.

   a. bored by the GravityLight

   b. excited about the GravityLight

2. Circle the clue(s) that helped you to make the inference in item 1.

   a. the speaker's speed and pitch

   b. the speaker's tone or laughter

   c. the speaker's descriptive words

3. In Excerpt 2, you can infer that the speaker is ____.

   a. excited about Mr. Trash Wheel

   b. disappointed that Mr. Trash Wheel has not collected more trash

4. Circle the clue(s) that helped you to make the inference in item 3.

   a. the speaker's speed and pitch

   b. the speaker's tone or laughter

   c. the speaker's descriptive words

iQ PRACTICE Go online for more practice listening to make inferences. *Practice > Unit 4 > Activity 6*

TIP FOR SUCCESS

Many tests require students to answer several inference questions. Learning to make inferences based on what you hear or read is an important part of preparing for tests.

ACADEMIC LANGUAGE

Sometimes speakers will tell you which information they feel is the most important by using phrases like these to draw listeners' attention to specific points:
the most important
most importantly
is important to
a very important
one of the key
one of the most

OPAL Oxford Phrasal Academic Lexicon

LISTENING 2 Moore's Law

OBJECTIVE ▶ You are going to watch a video and then listen to a related lecture. As you listen, gather information and ideas about how the laws of science affect our lives.

PREVIEW THE LISTENING

A. PREVIEW Moore's law predicted the small, fast technology that has resulted in the smartphones of today. If you were buying a new smartphone, what things would you consider? Look at the list. Check (✓) the things that are important to you.

- ☐ price
- ☐ screen size
- ☐ memory storage
- ☐ brand
- ☐ size
- ☐ speed
- ☐ battery life
- ☐ color

B. VOCABULARY Read aloud these words from Listening 2. Check (✓) the ones you know. Use a dictionary to define any new or unknown words. Then discuss with a partner how the words will relate to the unit.

astonishing *(adj.)* 🔑	**extent** *(n.)* 🔑 OPAL	**reflect** *(v.)* 🔑 OPAL
capacity *(n.)* 🔑 OPAL	**hilarious** *(adj.)* 🔑	**sophisticated** *(adj.)* 🔑
double *(v.)* 🔑	**noticeable** *(adj.)*	**target** *(n.)* 🔑 OPAL
dramatically *(adv.)* 🔑	**rapidly** *(adv.)* 🔑 OPAL	

🔑 Oxford 5000™ words   OPAL Oxford Phrasal Academic Lexicon

iQ PRACTICE Go online to listen and practice your pronunciation.
Practice › Unit 4 › Activity 7

WORK WITH THE LISTENING

iQ RESOURCES Go online to watch the video.
Resources > Video > Unit 4 > Listening 2

A. **LISTEN AND TAKE NOTES** Watch the video.* Then listen to the lecture. Take notes in the right section of the chart.

iQ RESOURCES Go online to download extra vocabulary support.
Resources > Extra Vocabulary > Unit 4

Questions	Notes on main ideas and important details

B. **COMPOSE** Read your notes and write questions about what you heard on the left.

C. **CATEGORIZE** Read the statements. Write *T* (true) or *F* (false). Then correct each false statement to make it true.

____ 1. Moore said the number of transistors that could fit on a circuit board would double every two years.

____ 2. The increase in transistors has doubled the price of computers.

____ 3. Experts do not believe we are approaching the end of Moore's law.

____ 4. MIT is working on a pill that turns a computer into medicine.

D. **IDENTIFY** Listening 2 mentions several different kinds of technology. Read the list below. Then watch and listen again and check (✓) which items you hear the speakers talk about.

☐ ATM   ☐ e-reader   ☐ smartwatch
☐ cell phone   ☐ GPS   ☐ tablet
☐ computer   ☐ laptop   ☐ virtual reality
☐ digital camera ☐ smartphone

*Audio version available. *Resources > Audio > Unit 4*

E. **IDENTIFY** Based on the listening, what might experts believe about Moore's law? Read the list and check (✓) the things that scientists might have said.

☐ 1. "Moore's law has had very little impact on the technology industry."

☐ 2. "The truth is that Moore's law has made amazing things possible."

☐ 3. "Cell phones would have been developed without the help of Moore's law. It might have just taken longer."

☐ 4. "Moore's law will last forever, making technology smaller and smaller in the future."

☐ 5. "The future of technology is really hard to predict because there is a clear limit to Moore's law."

☐ 6. "Moore's law has directly impacted the way we buy technology. We expect tech companies to introduce new, faster, smaller products every couple of years."

F. **DISCUSS** Share your answers with a partner. Discuss why you selected the answers you checked.

G. **DISCUSS** Work in a group to discuss the questions.

1. How has shrinking technology affected society? If computers were still the size of a room, how would life be different?

2. How might the computer pill that is being developed by MIT benefit people? Would you agree to try it? Why or why not?

VOCABULARY SKILL REVIEW

In Unit 3, you learned about checking the definitions of similar words to determine which word is appropriate in a context. Can you think of words that have meanings similar to *hilarious, rapidly,* or *sophisticated*? Look up those words in a dictionary and notice how their meanings are slightly different from the words in this list.

H. VOCABULARY Here are some words from Listening 2. Read the sentences. Then write each bold word next to the correct definition.

1. Prices have increased **dramatically** in the past few years. Everything is much more expensive than before.
2. The joke was **hilarious**. I couldn't stop laughing.
3. Computers are more **sophisticated** than they were even ten years ago. Technology has become very complex.
4. The change was really **noticeable** because it was so extreme.
5. **Double** all the ingredients in the recipe if you want to make the cake for twice as many people.
6. It's hard to understand the **extent** of the flood damage unless you see it from above in a helicopter.
7. It is **astonishing** how fast he can run. I just can't believe my eyes!
8. Cybersecurity is a **rapidly** growing industry. It seems as though new companies are opening every day.
9. The new policy **reflects** the company's new direction. It really shows what their values are.
10. The company set a **target** of making one million dollars in profit. They worked hard to meet it.
11. The stadium has a maximum **capacity** of over 50,000 people.

a. _____ (*adj.*) very funny

b. _____ (*v.*) to become or make something become twice as much or as many

c. _____ (*adj.*) easy to see or notice

d. _____ (*adj.*) very quickly

e. _____ (*adj.*) clever and complicated in the way that it works or is presented

f. _____ (*v.*) to show the nature of something or of someone's attitude or feeling

g. _____ (*adj.*) very surprising; difficult to believe

h. _____ (*n.*) how large, important, serious, etc., something is

i. _____ (*adv.*) very suddenly and to a very great and often surprising degree

j. _____ (*n.*) a result that you try to achieve

k. _____ (*n.*) amount that a container or space can hold

iQ PRACTICE Go online for more practice with the vocabulary.
Practice > Unit 4 > Activity 8

SAY WHAT YOU THINK

SYNTHESIZE Think about Listening 1 and Listening 2 as you discuss the questions.

1. How are Sir Isaac Newton and Gordon Moore similar, even though they lived 300 years apart?

2. The laws of science are based on observations about how nature works. Both listening texts show how this scientific knowledge can be used to change the world. What are other examples of science leading to important change?

VOCABULARY SKILL Word forms

Many words have several forms. For instance, a verb may have a noun form, an adjective form, and an adverb form. Notice all the forms of the verb *appreciate*.

- **Verb:** I **appreciate** all the help you have given us.
- **Noun:** We applauded to show our **appreciation**.
- **Adjective:** It feels great to lecture to an **appreciative** audience.
- **Adverb:** The children responded **appreciatively** when they received the gifts.

In some cases, different parts of speech of a word have the same form.

- **Noun:** John knew that he would never forget that **encounter** with the boss.
- **Verb:** When we arrive, I expect to **encounter** some problems.

When you look up a word in the dictionary, note its forms. This will help you build your vocabulary. Each word form will be marked with its part of speech. Common abbreviations for *verb, noun, adjective,* and *adverb* are *v., n., adj.,* and *adv*.

A. IDENTIFY Look at the verbs in bold. Circle the word on each line that is not a form of the bold verb. Use a dictionary to help you.

1. **produce** (*v.*):   productive   prodigy   productivity
2. **consider** (*v.*): consideration   considerate   consistent
3. **develop** (*v.*):   deviate   development   developer
4. **operate** (*v.*):   orate   operation   operator
5. **reflect** (*v.*):   reflection   reflex   reflective
6. **alternate** (*v.*): alternative   alternatively   altered

B. APPLY Complete the sentences with the correct form of the word in parentheses. Use a dictionary to help you.

1. You might wonder how a law of science is different from a _____ theory. (science, *adj.*)

2. _____, a law is something someone has observed about the world. (basic, *adv.*)

3. A law is always _____ and simple. (truth, *adj.*)

4. But, a theory is an _____ of why something happens. (explain, *n.*)

5. So, when Sir Isaac Newton observed the apple falling and _____ gravity, he was making a law. (description, *v.*)

6. But, scientists didn't really understand how gravity worked until Einstein _____ his theory of relativity. (development, *v.*)

iQ PRACTICE Go online for more practice using word forms.
Practice > Unit 4 > Activity 9

CRITICAL THINKING STRATEGY

Distinguishing between similar words

When you distinguish between things, you show you understand how things are different. This is a helpful skill to understand why a speaker chooses one word instead of another. For instance, if someone says a joke is funny, he or she probably smiled or laughed a little. However, if someone says a joke is hilarious, he or she probably laughed loudly and for a long time. Both *funny* and *hilarious* have the same basic meaning, but knowing the difference can help you understand more about the speaker's message.

iQ PRACTICE Go online to watch the Critical Thinking Video and check your comprehension. *Practice > Unit 4 > Activity 10*

C. IDENTIFY Read the sentences and match them with the correct message.

____ 1. I was **afraid**.　　　　　　a. It was a little scary, but I am fine.

____ 2. I was **terrified**.　　　　　b. It was so scary that I am still shaking.

____ 3. The car was **cheap**.　　　a. It was a good price. I can pay for it.

____ 4. The car was **affordable**.　b. The car was so inexpensive that I'm worried it will break down.

____ 5. I caught a **disease** on my trip.　a. I got seriously sick on vacation.

____ 6. I caught a **bug** on my trip.　　　b. I got a little sick on vacation.

SPEAKING

OBJECTIVE ▶ At the end of this unit, you are going to create a role-play about presenting a business plan for a new product. During the presentation, you will need to be able to politely avoid answering questions.

GRAMMAR Present perfect and present perfect continuous

Present Perfect

The **present perfect** can describe actions that happened at an unspecified time in the past. The present perfect construction is *has/have* + past participle.

> He **has worked** with the Waterfront Partnership of Baltimore to build a trash wheel.
> (They finished the trash wheel in the past, but we don't know exactly when.)

The present perfect also describes actions that started in the past and continue in the present time. The words *for* and *since* are used to describe actions that started at a definite time in the past.

> This city **has had** a problem with garbage in its harbor for many years.
> (The city started having the problem many years ago, and it still has the problem.)
> It's already **taken** more than a million pounds of trash out of the water.
> (It started taking trash out of the water when it was built, and it is still taking trash out of the water.)

The present perfect is often used to talk about past actions that happened more than once in the past.

> It **has** already **been** sold in countries like Kenya.
> (The company sold it multiple times in the recent past.)

Present Perfect Continuous

The **present perfect continuous** describes actions that started in the past but were not finished. By choosing the present perfect continuous, you are emphasizing that the action is continuing. The present perfect continuous construction is *has/have* + *been* + present participle.

> Many people around the world **have been using** kerosene lights.
> (They started using them in the past, and they are still using them.)
> John Kellett **has been working** for years in the harbor.
> (He started working in the harbor many years ago. He still works there.)

iQ RESOURCES Go online to watch the Grammar Skill Video.
Resources > Video > Unit 4 > Grammar Skill Video

A. APPLY Rewrite the sentences. Use the present perfect.

1. Alonzo started the project.

    Alonzo has started the project.

2. I thought a lot about this project over the past few years.

    _____

3. Ellen took several physics classes at the university.

    _____

4. Min-ju gave a sample of the product to her friends to test.

    _____

5. The company won three awards over the past year, and it will probably win more.

    _____

TIP FOR SUCCESS

When using present perfect and present perfect continuous verbs, speakers often contract *have* and *has* so they sound like *'ve* and *'s*. Listen for these contractions to help you understand a speaker's meaning.

B. IDENTIFY Complete the conversation. Circle the correct verb form. Then practice the conversation with a partner.

solar windows

Jamal: Hey, Ryan! Guess what? Rashida and I (have started / have been starting)¹ a new company recently. It's called Solectric.

Ryan: Oh, wow! That's great! What does your company do?

Jamal: Well, over the past couple of years, we (have worked / have been working)² on technology that focuses the sun so we can catch and keep the energy. We want to sell the technology to solar energy companies.

Ryan: Wait, what? How (have you come / have you been coming) up with that?
                                            3

Jamal: So, according to the first law of thermodynamics, energy can't be created or destroyed. It can only be changed. So we (have found / have been finding) a
                                                                                              4
way to use a special paint over normal window glass to catch the energy from the sun, make it stronger, save it, and change it into electricity.

Ryan: That's amazing! How much of the paint (have you sold / have you been selling) so far?
                                                                5

Jamal: We (have worked / have been working) on the product for years but just
                                            6
developed the sales presentation last week.

Ryan: That's great news, Jamal!

iQ PRACTICE Go online for more practice with the present perfect and present perfect continuous. *Practice > Unit 4 > Activity 11*

iQ PRACTICE Go online for the Grammar Expansion: future forms: *will, be going to,* and future continuous. *Practice > Unit 4 > Activity 12*

PRONUNCIATION Basic intonation patterns

Intonation Pattern

When you are speaking, the pitch of your voice goes up and down. This change in pitch is called an **inonation pattern**. Intonation patterns carry a lot of information. For instance, your intonation will let your listener know if you are asking a question or making a statement. It's important to use the correct intonation pattern to effectively communicate your meaning.

Rising/Falling

One of the most common intonation patterns in English is the *rising/falling* pattern, where the pitch rises before the last word and falls on the last word. This pattern is common in simple declarative sentences, direct commands, and *wh-* questions.

I enjoyed it very much.
Hand me that brush, please.
What have you seen?

Rising

For *yes/no* questions, use a rising intonation pattern.

Are you concerned?

🔊 **A. ANALYZE** Listen to each sentence. Write *R* (rising intonation pattern) or *RF* (rising/falling pattern). Then repeat each sentence.

____ 1. Gordon Moore made an important prediction.

____ 2. Where did he work?

____ 3. Did Moore's law create new industries?

____ 4. What has Moore's law changed?

____ 5. Will Moore's law continue forever?

____ 6. Computers are not rare and expensive anymore.

____ 7. Can you imagine a day without your smartphone?

____ 8. How do you feel about computers being able to read your mind?

🔊 **B. APPLY** Listen to the conversation. Draw arrows to show the intonation patterns. Listen again and repeat. Then practice the conversation with a partner.

Alex: What's that?

Lee: It's a cool new flashlight.

Alex: What's so cool about it?

Lee: The power for it comes from the heat of my hand.

Alex: How does that work?

Lee: It's the thermoelectric effect. It changes the heat into electricity.

Alex: Can I see it?

Lee: Here you are.

Alex: It really works!

iQ PRACTICE Go online for more practice with basic intonation patterns.
Practice › Unit 4 › Activity 13

SPEAKING SKILL Avoiding answering questions

There are times when you prefer not to answer a question that someone has asked you. Here are several ways that you can avoid answering questions without being impolite.

Refuse politely.

> A: Who did you vote for?
> B: Actually, I'd prefer not to say.

> A: How have your sales been so far this year?
> B: Sorry, but we're not ready to release that information.

Ask another question.

> A: What do you think of the new CEO?
> B: What do you think?

Answer a different question.

You can provide related information without addressing the question that was actually asked.

> A: Are you looking for a new job?
> B: I like this job very much.

Use vague phrases.

Phrases like *you might say* or *one could conclude* avoid stating your own opinion directly.

> A: What do you think about the new smartphone?
> B: You might say it's a good product for some people.

Refusing politely is the simplest and most direct way to avoid answering a question. Using vague phrases is the least direct way. These strategies can be used in all types of situations.

A. CATEGORIZE Listen to the conversations. With a partner, discuss what strategy each speaker uses to avoid answering a question. Then practice the conversations with your partner.

1. A: How old are you?

    B: I'd rather not say.

2. A: What did you think of the company president's speech?

    B: You might say it gives a very unique point of view.

3. A: Hello. Is Nick there?

    B: Who's calling?

4. A: Is Joseph doing a good job?

   B: Joseph is a very hard worker.

5. A: Can I have your address, please?

   B: I'm sorry, but I don't give out that information.

6. A: Where were you on Friday?

   B: Why do you need to know?

B. COMPOSE Read the questions. Write responses that avoid answering the questions directly. Then practice with a partner.

1. A: Would you like to invest in our new company, Solectric?

   B: _____

2. A: What do you think of the new heat-powered flashlight?

   B: _____

3. A: Would you like information on our latest products?

   B: _____

4. A: What is your email address?

   B: _____

iQ PRACTICE Go online for more practice avoiding answering questions. Practice > Unit 4 > Activity 14

UNIT ASSIGNMENT Present a business plan
OBJECTIVE ▶

In this assignment, you are going to create a role-play about presenting a business plan for a new product. Your classmates will be potential investors in your business. As you prepare your presentation, think about the Unit Question, "How do the laws of science affect our lives?" Use information from Listening 1, Listening 2, and your work in this unit to support your presentation. Refer to the Self-Assessment checklist on page 100.

CONSIDER THE IDEAS

What kinds of science-based products would you be interested in making or selling? Consider the products you have heard about in this unit, the information below, and any other products related to the laws of science you can think of. Discuss these questions in a group.

1. What kinds of products do you think would sell well? Why? Who would buy them?

2. Would you be willing to invest money to support someone's business that was making the following products? Why or why not?

   a. **Vibeat:** Headphones that convert sound into vibration so the deaf can experience music (law of reflection)

   b. **Fly-bot:** Tiny drone that processes what it "sees" very rapidly, allowing it to move quickly in dangerous situations (Moore's law)

   c. **Synthetic jet propulsion system:** Lighter pieces of a rocket that reduce the amount of fuel a rocket needs to take off (Newton's third law of motion)

   d. **Floating trash collector:** Tubes in the ocean that collect garbage and don't hurt fish (Archimedes's buoyancy principle)

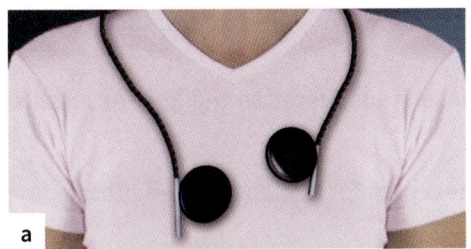
a

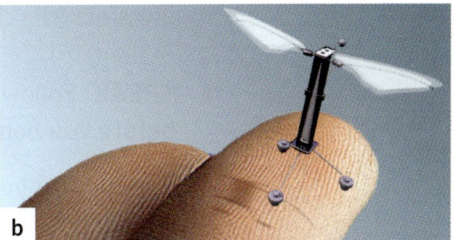
b

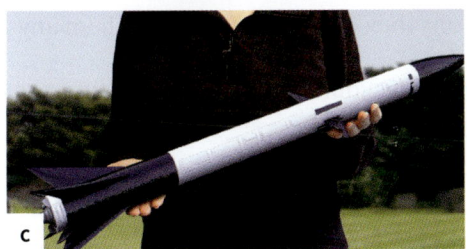
c

d

PREPARE AND SPEAK

A. GATHER IDEAS Read the list of questions an investor might ask an entrepreneur before lending him or her money to start a new business. Add questions based on your discussion in the Consider the Ideas activity.

You and the product

1. What makes the product that you are selling unique?

2. How much experience do you have running a business?

3. _____

   The market

4. Who will you sell your product to? That is, who is your target market?

5. Who else sells products like yours? That is, who is your competition?

6. _____

The deal

7. How much does it cost to make the product, and how much will you sell it for?

8. How much money do you want from an investor to help start your business?

9. _____

B. ORGANIZE IDEAS Choose a science-based product for which you would like to develop a business plan and get investors.

1. Prepare responses to the questions in Activity A. Are there any questions in the list you might want to avoid answering? How will you avoid answering them?

2. Think about your presentation. How will you make it interesting for potential investors (the class) and capture their attention?

C. SPEAK Follow these steps. Refer to the Self-Assessment checklist below before you begin.

1. Present your business plan for a science-based product to potential investors (the class).

2. Answer any questions they might have, and ask them any questions you have.

iQ PRACTICE Go online for your alternate Unit Assignment.
Practice > Unit 4 > Activity 15

CHECK AND REFLECT

A. CHECK Think about the Unit Assignment as you complete the Self-Assessment checklist.

SELF-ASSESSMENT	Yes	No
I was able to speak easily about the topic.	☐	☐
My partner, group, and class understood me.	☐	☐
I used the present perfect and the present perfect continuous.	☐	☐
I used vocabulary from the unit.	☐	☐
I used strategies to avoid answering questions.	☐	☐
I used correct intonation patterns.	☐	☐

B. REFLECT Discuss these questions with a partner or group.

1. What is something new you learned in this unit?

2. Look back at the Unit Question—How do the laws of science affect our lives? Is your answer different now than it was when you started this unit? If yes, how is it different? Why?

iQ PRACTICE Go to the online discussion board to discuss the questions. *Practice > Unit 4 > Activity 16*

TRACK YOUR SUCCESS

iQ PRACTICE Go online to check the words and phrases you have learned in this unit. *Practice > Unit 4 > Activity 17*

Check (✓) the skills and strategies you learned. If you need more work on a skill, refer to the page(s) in parentheses.

NOTE-TAKING	☐ I can use a split page to take notes and create questions. (p. 80)
LISTENING	☐ I can make inferences. (p. 85)
VOCABULARY	☐ I can use word forms. (p. 91)
CRITICAL THINKING	☐ I can distinguish between similar words. (p. 92)
GRAMMAR	☐ I can use the present perfect and the present perfect continuous. (p. 93)
PRONUNCIATION	☐ I can use basic intonation patterns. (p. 95)
SPEAKING	☐ I can avoid answering questions. (p. 97)
OBJECTIVE ▶	☐ I can gather information and ideas to create a role-play about presenting a business plan for a new product.

VOCABULARY LIST AND CEFR CORRELATION

🔑 The **Oxford 5000**™ is an expanded core word list for advanced learners of English. The words have been chosen based on their frequency in the Oxford English Corpus and relevance to learners of English. As well as the **Oxford 3000**™ core word list, the Oxford 5000 includes an additional 2,000 words that are aligned to the CEFR, guiding advanced learners at B2–C1 level on the most useful high-level words to learn to expand their vocabulary.

OPAL The **Oxford Phrasal Academic Lexicon** is an essential guide to the most important words and phrases to know for academic English. The word lists are based on the Oxford Corpus of Academic English and the British Academic Spoken English corpus.

The **Common European Framework of Reference for Language (CEFR)** provides a basic description of what language learners have to do to use language effectively. The system contains 6 reference levels: A1, A2, B1, B2, C1, C2.

UNIT 1

advance (v.) 🔑 B2
assess (v.) 🔑 OPAL B2
capable (adj.) 🔑 OPAL B2
clarity (n.) 🔑 C1
contact (n.) 🔑 OPAL B1
effective (adj.) 🔑 OPAL B1
enthusiasm (n.) 🔑 B2
ethical (adj.) 🔑 OPAL B2
executive (n.) 🔑 B2
initiative (n.) 🔑 OPAL B2
innovation (n.) 🔑 B2
motivation (n.) 🔑 OPAL B2
perspective (n.) 🔑 OPAL B2
promote (v.) 🔑 OPAL B1
realistic (adj.) 🔑 B2
responsibility (n.) 🔑 OPAL B1
role (n.) 🔑 OPAL A2
style (n.) 🔑 OPAL A1
take on (v. phr.) 🔑 B1
title (n.) 🔑 OPAL A1
versus (prep.) 🔑 OPAL C1

UNIT 2

bias (n.) 🔑 OPAL B2
chaos (n.) 🔑 C1
embrace (v.) 🔑 B2
feature (n.) 🔑 OPAL A2
grant (v.) 🔑 B2
imply (v.) 🔑 OPAL B2
inflexible (adj.) C1
legal (adj.) 🔑 OPAL B1
manufacture (v.) 🔑 B2

moderately (adv.) C1
monopoly (n.) 🔑 C1
obtain (v.) 🔑 OPAL B2
open-minded (adj.) C1
point out (v. phr.) 🔑 B1
purchase (n.) 🔑 B2
recognize (v.) 🔑 OPAL A2
revert (v.) C2
shade (n.) 🔑 B2
stifle (v.) C1
stimulating (adj.) B2
stumble upon (v. phr.) C2
theme (n.) 🔑 OPAL B1
trademark (v.) 🔑 C1
turn out (v. phr.) 🔑 B1

UNIT 3

agency (n.) 🔑 B2
asset (n.) 🔑 B2
balance (v.) 🔑 OPAL B1
current (adj.) 🔑 OPAL B1
debt (n.) 🔑 B2
entrepreneur (n.) 🔑 B2
insurance (n.) 🔑 B2
interest (n.) 🔑 OPAL A1
minor (adj.) 🔑 OPAL B2
mortgage (n.) 🔑 B2
naturally (adv.) 🔑 OPAL B1
nutrition (n.) 🔑 B2
pension (n.) 🔑 B2
precisely (adv.) 🔑 OPAL B2
retirement (n.) 🔑 B2
series (n.) 🔑 OPAL A2

set up (v. phr.) 🔑 B1
spare (n.) C1
stock (n.) 🔑 OPAL B2
tool (n.) 🔑 OPAL A2
tedious (adj.) C1
truly (adv.) 🔑 B2
weigh in (v. phr.) C2

UNIT 4

affordable (adj.) 🔑 B2
alternative (n.) 🔑 OPAL A2
astonishing (adj.) 🔑 B2
capacity (n.) 🔑 OPAL B2
double (v.) 🔑 A2
dramatically (adv.) 🔑 B2
extent (n.) 🔑 OPAL B2
force (n.) 🔑 OPAL B1
function (v.) 🔑 OPAL B2
gear (n.) 🔑 C1
hazardous (adj.) C1
hilarious (adj.) 🔑 B2
intention (n.) 🔑 OPAL B1
inventor (n.) B1
noticeable (adj.) C1
power (v.) 🔑 B2
rapidly (adv.) 🔑 OPAL B2
reflect (v.) 🔑 OPAL B1
sophisticated (adj.) 🔑 B2
stream (v.) C1
summarize (v.) 🔑 OPAL B1
target (n.) 🔑 OPAL A2
throughout (prep.) 🔑 OPAL B1